GREAT SCENES AND

MONOLOGUES

For
Children

Smith and Kraus *Books For Actors*

YOUNG ACTORS SERIES
New Plays from A.C.T.'s Young Conservatory
Great Scenes for Young Actors from the Stage
Great Monologues for Young Actors

THE MONOLOGUE SERIES
The Best Men's / Women's Stage Monologues of 1992
The Best Men's / Women's Stage Monologues of 1991
The Best Men's / Women's Stage Monologues of 1990
One Hundred Men's / Women's Stage Monologues from the 1980's
Street Talk: Character Monologues for Actors
Uptown: Character Monologues for Actors
Monologues from Contemporary Literature: Volume I
Monologues from Classic Plays
Kiss and Tell: The Art of the Restoration Monologue

FESTIVAL MONOLOGUE SERIES
The Great Monologues from the Humana Festival
The Great Monologues from the EST Marathon
The Great Monologues from the Women's Project
The Great Monologues from the Mark Taper Forum

SCENE STUDY SERIES
The Best Stage Scenes for Women from the 1980's
The Best Stage Scenes for Men from the 1980's
The Best Stage Scenes of 1992

PLAYS FOR ACTORS SERIES
Seventeen Short Plays by Romulus Linney
Lanford Wilson: 21 Short Plays
William Mastrosimone: Collected Plays
Eric Overmyer: Collected Plays
Terrence McNally: Collected Plays

GREAT TRANSLATIONS FOR ACTORS SERIES
The Wood Demon by Anton Chekhov

OTHER BOOKS IN OUR COLLECTION
The Actor's Chekhov
Women Playwrights: The Best Plays of 1992
Humana Festival '93: The Collected Plays
Break A Leg! Daily Inspiration for the Actor

If you require pre-publication information about upcoming Smith and Kraus books, you may receive our semi-annual catalogue, free of charge, by sending your name and address to *Smith and Kraus Catalogue, P.O. Box 127, Lyme, NH 03768 (800) 895-4331, FAX (603) 795-4427.*

GREAT SCENES AND MONOLOGUES

For
Children

Craig Slaight and Jack Sharrar, editors

The Young Actors Series

SK
A Smith and Kraus Book

A Smith and Kraus Book
Published by Smith and Kraus, Inc.

COVER AND TEXT DESIGN BY JULIA HILL
Manufactured in the United States of America

First Edition: March 1993
10 9 8 7 6 5 4 3 2

Library of Congress Cataloging-in-Publication Data
Great scenes and monologues for children / edited by Craig Slaight and Jack Sharrar. --1st ed.
         p. cm.
     Summary: Presents a collection of monologues and scenes from familiar plays and books for young actors to perform.
         ISBN 1-880399-15-6
         1. Monologues--Juvenile literature. 2. Acting--Juvenile literature. [1. Monologues. 2. Acting.] I. Slaight, Craig. II. Sharrar, Jack F., 1949-
PN2080.G727   1993   93-15723
808.82'45--dc20   CIP
                                             AC

For Stacy and For Howard

It is only with the heart that one can see rightly;
what is essential is invisible to the eye.

The Fox from
The Little Prince
by Antoine de Saint Exupéry

CRAIG SLAIGHT is the director of the Young Conservatory at the American Conservatory Theater in San Francisco. Prior to joining A.C.T., Mr. Slaight was head of the acting and directing program at the Los Angeles County High School for the Arts. He also served on the theater faculty at the Interlochen Center for the Arts. In addition to his commitment to developing and training young actors, Mr. Slaight spent ten years in Los Angeles as a professional director. He currently serves on the Territorial Board of the Educational Theatre Association and is a member of the Theater Panel for ARTS, sponsored by the National Foundation for Advancement in the Arts. He is co-editor (with Jack Sharrar) of *Great Scenes for Young Actors from the Stage* and *Great Monologues for Young Actors.*

JACK SHARRAR is Registrar and Director of Alumni Relations for the American Conservatory Theater, where he also teaches acting, directing, and voice. Mr. Sharrar is a graduate of the University of Michigan, and holds a Ph.D. in theater history and dramatic literature from the University of Utah. He is author of *Avery Hopwood, His Life and Plays*; contributor to Oxford University Press's *The American National Biography*, and co-author (with Craig Slaight) of *Great Scenes for Young Actors from the Stage* and *Great Monologues for Young Actors*, which the New York Public Library recognized as one of the Best Books for the Teenage 1993.

Contents

MONOLOGUES FOR GIRLS

MONOLOGUES FOR BOYS

Acknowledgments

The editors wish to express their thanks to Horton Foote, Timothy Mason, Judy Johnson Wilson, the students and staff of the American Conservatory Theater, and especially to Marisa and Eric, for their assistance in preparing this collection.

Introduction

You are reading this book because the art of theater and drama is important in your life. Perhaps you are just beginning to discover the value and excitement of seeing a well-told story performed live on a stage by actors before an audience, or maybe you have already acted such stories yourself before people who share your love of theater and drama. This new found love you feel for telling stories through drama is as old as mankind. It connects you through history to a living art that helps us better understand what it means to be a human being in a dynamic world of varied cultures and unique environments.

The scenes and monologues included in this book have been selected to help you on your journey of discovery. All of the material is seen through the eyes of young people such as yourself. You will find that some of the material we chose was not written for the stage, however, such as selections from novels and short stories, or in one instance, a personal letter. This material allows for exciting dramatic discovery nonetheless. Through these stories and characters created by playwrights and writers of other kinds of literature, you will begin to develop a greater appreciation of the power of theater and drama in our lives.

As you explore the material in this book, we hope that you will take the time to find the complete works, and read them, too. For only after reading an entire work, can you begin to fully understand and develop the characters you have chosen to play. Welcome to the art of drama and theater. We hope that your love continues to grow.

Craig Slaight
Jack Sharrar
San Francisco, CA
March, 1993

Scenes
For
Children

Mark Twain's
THE ADVENTURES OF TOM SAWYER
Adapted for the Stage by Timothy Mason

The Characters: Tom (10-12) and Becky (10-12)

Mark Twain's memorable and timeless story of growing up in the south mixes young love and mischievousness, suspense and... adventure. Tom is a character that might live in any time. As we follow his life, we are treated to a glimpse of another time in history, but a time that features getting in trouble, falling in love, making important decisions and having fun!

In this first scene, Tom finally gets the opportunity, at school, to try to win the affections of beautiful, blue-eyed Becky Thatcher.

TOM: Do you like rats?

BECKY: Rats? Of course not! I hate them!

TOM: *(Switching tactics.)* Oh! Well, o'course, I hate 'em, too. *Live* ones. But I mean, dead ones, to swing around yer head with a string.

BECKY: No, I mostly don't care for rats either way. What *I* like is chewing gum.

TOM: Oh, I should say so! I wisht I had some right now.

BECKY: Do you? I've got some. I'll let you chew it awhile, but you have to give it back.

(The wad of chewing gum changes hands furtively.)

TOM: It's all right. Nobody's lookin'. Say, Becky, was you ever engaged?

BECKY: What?

TOM: Engaged to be married.

BECKY: Why, no.

TOM: Would you like to?

BECKY: I suppose so. I don't know. What's it like?

TOM: Like? Why it ain't like anything. You only just tell a boy that you love him forever and ever, and then you kiss and that's all there is to it. Shoot. It's easy.

BECKY: What do you have to kiss for?

TOM: Why, that's, *you* know – well, they *always* do it.

BECKY: Everybody?

TOM: Why, sure! Come on, say you love me.

BECKY: No!

TOM: Please?

BECKY: ... Tomorrow.

TOM: No, *now*. Just whisper it, that's all.

BECKY: Well, you turn your face away so you can't see. And you mustn't ever tell anybody – will you, Tom? Ever?
(Tom shakes his head, Becky leans close to his ear and whispers.)

TOM: Hooo-ee! Now it's all over but the kiss, and that ain't nothin' at all.
(Tom raises Becky's slate in front of their faces and they kiss behind it.)
See? Ain't it nice to be engaged?

BECKY: Oh, Tom, it's ever so nice! I never even heard of it before.

TOM: Oh, shoot. It's lots of fun. Why, when me and Amy Lawrence was engag...
(Tom suddenly realizes his blunder.)

BECKY: Oh, Tom! You mean I ain't the first girl you've ever been engaged to?
(She bursts into tears.)

TOM: Don't cry, Becky! Me and Amy, we wasn't *really* engaged, not like you and me...

In this second scene, Tom and Becky have lost their way, deep in a dark, damp and spooky cave. Separated from their friends, looking for a way out, their nerves are on edge.

(The sound of dripping water echoes and intensifies. A flutter of bat wings passes by. Finally, a match is struck in the darkness, and a candle is lit. An isolated pool of light grows around Tom and Becky Thatcher.)

BECKY: Please don't let it go out like that again, Tom. I do wish we hadn't let the others get so far ahead of us.

TOM: It don't matter, Becky. I know my way.

BECKY: I cain't hear 'em anymore, Tom. Can you?

(Pause while they listen. Then there is a faint, echoing laugh.)

TOM: There! You hear that? Now we just follow that voice…down this way, I reckon…

(They begin to descend. Suddenly, a distant echoing curse from a different direction. Tom and Becky stop.)

BECKY: Oh, Tom! Everything's mixed up in here.

TOM: Now that voice were above us…and to the right, I think. Just take my hand, Becky.

(Tom leads her up again in the direction they just came from.)

This here might be the passage…

(They start into it and we lose sight of them. Tom shouts.)

Hello! –ello –ello –ello –ello…

BECKY: Don't shout so, Tom! It makes such a horrid noise.

(They come into view again at another location.)

TOM: I know, Becky, but it just might be they'll be able to hear us.

BECKY: *Might* be? Oh, Tom…Tom, I'm scared…

TOM: It's all right, Becky. The others'll be sure to miss us…

BECKY: Yes. Yes, they'll miss us and they'll start huntin' for us…

TOM: Why, shore they will.

BECKY: Maybe they're huntin' for us right now, Tom!

TOM: I…I reckon, maybe they are.

BECKY: *(A hint of growing hysteria.)* They're probably lookin'… they're lookin' all over, right now…for us…and they're a-shoutin' for us and…

(Mood shift.)

Tom, I don't hear no shouting…they ain't lookin' for us at all, Tom…They don't even know we're *lost,* Tom, they don't even *know*…

TOM: Shhht! What was that?

(Silence. Then, echoing footsteps. The footsteps suddenly stop.)

BECKY: Tom! Tom, it's them!

(Becky breaks away from Tom and runs blindly in the direction of the sound.)

Hello? Help! Help!

TOM: Becky, come back!

(He runs after her, trips and falls in the dark.)

BECKY: I see a light, Tom! We're saved! Hello! Over here! We're over here! Becky Thatcher and Tom Sawyer!

(Becky is groping her way frantically in the darkness. Tom gets

to his feet and tries to follow her.)

TOM: Becky, stop! You'll fall off a ledge up there! Wait for me!

BECKY: Oh, Tom! I cain't see it no more! The candle! It was coming towards us and now it's gone!

TOM: *(Catching up to her.)* Wait, Becky!

(Injun Joe leaps out from behind a rock barrier.)

BECKY: *(A scream.)*

ALICE'S ADVENTURES IN WONDERLAND
Adapted by Craig Slaight
From the novel by Lewis Carroll

The Characters: Alice (11) and the Cheshire Cat (ageless)

Lewis Carroll's timeless classic creates a world of make-believe where anything can happen and often does. Little Alice tumbles into a most fantastic place and she meets some of the most unusual inhabitants one could ever imagine: the White Rabbit, the March Hare and Mad Hatter, the Caterpillar, Tweedledum and Tweedledee, the Queen of Hearts, and, of course, Humpty Dumpty, to name a few. Alice has a remarkable visit and returns to her own world a little bit smarter than when she left.

In the first scene below, Alice has lost her way, when suddenly the grinning Cheshire Cat appears before her. She seeks its help.

(As Alice walks, thinking, she is startled by seeing a cat with long claws and large teeth sitting on a branch of a tree. The cat has an extraordinary grin.)

ALICE: Cheshire Puss, would you tell me, please, which way I ought to walk from here?

CAT: That depends a good deal on where you want to get to.

ALICE: I don't much care where...

CAT: Then it doesn't matter which way you walk.

ALICE: As long as I get *somewhere.*

CAT: Oh, you're sure to do that if you only walk long enough.

ALICE: What sort of people live here?

CAT: (*Waves right paw around.*) In *that* direction, lives a Hatter; (*Waves the other paw.*) and in *that* direction, lives a March Hare. Visit either you like; they're both mad.

ALICE: But I don't want to go among mad people.

CAT: You can't help that. We're all mad here. I'm mad. You're mad.

ALICE: How do you know that I'm mad?

CAT: You must be or you wouldn't have come here.

ALICE: And how do you know that you're mad?

CAT: To begin with, a dog's not mad. You grant that?

ALICE: I suppose so.

CAT: Well then, you see a dog growls when it's angry, and wags its tail when it's pleased. Now *I* growl when I'm pleased, and wag my tail when I'm angry. Therefore I'm mad.

ALICE: *I* call it purring, not growling.

CAT: Call it what you like. Do you play croquet with the Queen today?

ALICE: I should like it very much but I haven't been invited yet.

CAT: You'll see me there.

(The Cat vanishes. Alice stands bewildered, not knowing how or where the cat has vanished. The Cat reappears.)

By-the-bye, what became of the baby? I'd nearly forgotten to ask.

ALICE: It turned into a pig.

CAT: I thought it would.

(Once again he vanishes. Alice waits again for the Cat to reappear. When she is convinced that it will not reappear, she walks on.)

ALICE: *(To herself:)* I've seen Hatters before, the March Hare will be much the most interesting, and perhaps as this is May it won't be raving mad - at least not so mad as it was in March.

(Alice looks up where she is and suddenly, the Cat is there.)

CAT: Did you say pig, or fig?

ALICE: I said pig and I wish you wouldn't keep appearing and vanishing so suddenly; you make one quite giddy.

CAT: All right. *(He vanishes very slowly, until he's gone. All that remains is his grin, which doesn't fade.)*

ALICE: Well, I've often seen a cat without a grin, but a grin without a cat! It's the most curious thing I ever saw in all my life!

The Characters: Alice (11) and the Caterpillar (ageless)

In the scene below, Alice discovers a caterpillar sitting atop a mushroom tall, leisurely puffing on a hookah, a large water pipe.

(The Caterpillar and Alice look at each other in silence. Finally, the Caterpillar takes the hookah out of his mouth and speaks to Alice.)

CATERPILLAR: Who are *you*?

ALICE: (*Shyly.*) I – I hardly know, sir, just at present - at least I know who I *was* when I got up this morning, but I must have changed several times since then.

CATERPILLAR: What do you mean by that? Explain yourself.

ALICE: I can't explain *myself*, I'm afraid, sir, because I'm not myself, you see.

CATERPILLAR: I don't see.

ALICE: (*Politely.*) I'm afraid I can't put it more clearly, for I can't understand it myself to begin with; and being so many different sizes in a day is very confusing.

CATERPILLAR: It isn't.

ALICE: Well, perhaps you haven't found it so yet, but when you have to turn into a chrysalis - you will some day, you know - and then after that into a butterfly, I should think you'll feel it a little queer, won't you?

CATERPILLAR: Not a bit.

ALICE: Well, perhaps your feelings may be different; all I know is, it would feel very queer to *me*.

CATERPILLAR: You! Who are you?

ALICE: (*She tries to control her anger.*) I think you ought to tell me who you are first.

CATERPILLAR: Why?

(*A long pause. Finally, Alice starts to leave.*)

Come back! I've something important to say.

(*Alice stops, turns, and decides to come back.*)

Keep your temper.

ALICE: Is that all?

CATERPILLAR: No.

(*The Caterpillar doesn't speak for awhile, puffing on his hookah. Finally, the Caterpillar takes the hookah out of his mouth and says:*)

So you think you're changed, do you?

ALICE: I'm afraid I am, sir. I can't remember things as I used, and I don't keep the same size for ten minutes together!

CATERPILLAR: What size do you want to be?

ALICE: Oh, I'm not particular as to size, only one doesn't like changing so often, you know.

CATERPILLAR: I *don't* know.

(*Alice says nothing to this.*)

CATERPILLAR: Are you content now?

ALICE: Well I should like to be a *little* larger, sir, if you wouldn't mind. Three inches is such a wretched height to be.

CATERPILLAR: (*Angered by this, for he is only three inches tall, he rises on the mushroom:*) It is a very good height indeed!

ALICE: (*Attempting to calm him.*) But I'm not used to it! (*Aside.*) I wish the creatures wouldn't be so easily offended!

CATERPILLAR: You'll get used to it in time.

(*The Caterpillar begins to smoke again, while Alice waits. Finally he speaks as he crawls off the mushroom.*)
One side will make you grow taller, and the other side will make you grow shorter.

ALICE: (*Thinks about this. Then, to herself:*) One side of *what*? The other side of *what*?

CATERPILLAR: (*As he slides away as if he has heard Alice:*) Of the mushroom.

(*Alice, perplexed by this, tries to figure out the two sides of the mushroom, which of course is round. Finally she breaks off a piece from the back and a piece from the edge.*)

ALICE: And now which is which?

(*She tastes a piece from the right hand bit. A sudden blow is felt under her chin. She is shrinking fast. To counter the effect, she tastes from the other bit.*)

APPROACHING ZANZIBAR
by Tina Howe

The Characters: Pony (9) and Turner (12)

The Blossom family are traveling by car across the country to visit
Charlotte Blossom's dying aunt in Taos, New Mexico. Along the way,
everyone in the family experiences something important, especially
eighty-one year old Aunt Olivia. Here the young people help the old
sort out their lives.

In the first scene, Pony and her brother Turner awake at their
campsite to find that Charlotte and Matthew (Mom and Dad) are gone.
They haven't gone far, but Pony and Turner don't know that. It is that
late, scary time of night.)

PONY: *(Wakes like a shot.)* What was that?
   *(Silence. Then all the sounds combine into a terrifying
   cacophony.)*
PONY: *(In a whisper.)* Mommy?
   (The sounds get louder…)
PONY: Mommy…?!
   (…And louder.)
PONY: *(Frozen.)* It's bears!
   (Dead silence.)
PONY: MOOOOOOMMYYYYYYYYY???!
TURNER: *(Wakes instantly.)* What's happening?
PONY: It's bears. Big black bears!
   (Silence.)
TURNER: I don't hear anything.
   (The lion roars again.)
TURNER: *(Whispering.)* Dad…?
PONY: *(Whispering.)* Mommy…?
TURNER: Is that you?
PONY: Can I get in with you?
TURNER: It's so dark in here.
PONY: *(Creeping out of her sleeping bag.)* Where are you?
TURNER: *(Likewise.)* Who has the flashlight?
PONY: Mommy…?

TURNER: *(Running into her.)* Dad…?

PONY: No, it's me, Pony.

TURNER: *Pony…?*

PONY: What?

TURNER: Oh, no!

PONY: *Turner…?*

TURNER: Where are they?
(Silence.)

TURNER and PONY: DAD…? MOMMY? …MOOOMMYY?
(Silence.)

PONY: *The bears got them, the bears got them!*

TURNER: Will you shut up?

PONY: I want Mommy, I want Mommy!

TURNER: Come on, quiet down or they'll get us, too!
(An instant silence.)

PONY: *(Jumping.)* What was that?

TURNER: What was what?

PONY: *That!?*

TURNER: I didn't hear anything.

PONY: It sounded like snakes.

TURNER: Will you stop it?

PONY: It's snakes, it's snakes!

TURNER: Wait a minute, let me get my circus light.
(He turns on one of those little fibre optic flashlights they sell at circuses and starts waving it, drawing liquid circles in the air.)

PONY: Oh, neat! Let me try.

TURNER: Use your own.

PONY: I don't know where it is.

TURNER: Look in your sleeping bag.
(He keeps waving it.)

PONY: Hey, I found it, I found it!
(She turns her flashlight on and copies Turner.)
This is fun.

TURNER: I wish we had sparklers.

PONY: Oh, sparklers would be great!
(They wave away until the tent starts to glow.)

PONY: Hey, why don't you play your guitar.

TURNER: Now?

PONY: It would be neat.

TURNER: Yeah?

PONY: Yeah, we'll have a sound-and-light show. I'll do them both and you play that really beautiful piece...

TURNER: *(With enthusiasm.)* Okaaay!

(He hands her his light and starts taking his guitar out of its case.)

PONY: Are you scared of seeing Livvie?

TURNER: Why should I be scared?

PONY: Because she's dying of cancer.

TURNER: So?

PONY: She'll look all strange. Her teeth will be black and she'll be wearing a wig.

TURNER: How do you know?

PONY: I heard Mommy and Daddy talking.

(Turner starts playing Bach's Suite No. 1 in G major. Pony listens for several measures, then resumes waving the lights as Turner plays.)

PONY: What if she dies in front of us? What if she turns blue and starts gasping for air...?

(She makes lurid strangling sounds.)

What if she wants to be alone with one of us? What if we're locked in a room with her and she comes after us...? What if she falls and dies right on top of us...?

(There's a sudden awful noise outside.)

PONY: *(Dropping the lights.)* IT'S HER, IT'S HER...SHE'S COMING TO GET US!

(Turner continues playing.)

HELP...HELP...!

TURNER: *(Stops playing.)* Jeez, Pony!

PONY: She's coming to get us, she's coming to get us!

TURNER: She lives over 2,000 miles away!

PONY: Mommy, Mommy...!

TURNER: *(Rising.)* I'm getting out of here, you're crazy!

PONY: Hey, where are you going?

TURNER: *(Heading for the door.)* I want to see what's going on.

PONY: You can't go out there.

TURNER: Who says?

PONY: The bears will get you! *(In a frantic whisper.)* Turner...?!

TURNER: *(Pulls back the tent flap and steps outside.)* Ohhh, look at all those stars!

(Moonlight pours through the door.)

PONY: Turner, get back in here!

TURNER: The sky's full of shooting stars. Quick, Pone, you've got to see this!

PONY: *(Whimpering.)* I want Mommy, I want Mommy...

TURNER: *(Returning for Pony.)* They're amazing. Come on, give me your hand.

PONY: Where are we going?

TURNER: Just follow me.

(He leads her to a clearing outside the tent. The sky is ablaze with shooting stars. He puts his arm around her shoulder.)

Well, what do you think?

PONY: Ohhhh, look!

TURNER: Isn't it incredible?

PONY: Look at all those stars!

TURNER: *(Pointing.)* Oh, one's falling, one's falling!

PONY: There are millions of them...

TURNER: Did you see that?

PONY: ...billions and zillions of them!

TURNER: Come on, let's get closer.

PONY: Ohhh, they're so bright!

(Arms around each other, they walk out into the starlit night.)

TURNER: Hold on tight now. I don't want to lose you.

The Characters: Pony (9) and Olivia (adult)

In this scene, Pony is left alone to visit Aunt Olivia.

OLIVIA: *(Closes her eyes, then opens them and smiles.)*

There, this is more like it. Sit down, sit down.

(Pony pulls up a chair next to her and sits. Olivia casually plucks an orchid out of her vase and starts eating it.)

Mmmm...

(Pony watches, amazed.)

Would you like to try one?

PONY: Could I?

OLIVIA: *(Handing it to her.)* Please!

PONY: *(Takes a cautious bite.)* Mmmm, I've never had this kind before.

(She eats with rising gusto.)

OLIVIA: They're orchids.

PONY: *(Finishing it off.)* It's so sweet!

OLIVIA: An old admirer sends them to me from Hawaii. Here, have some more.

(She hands Pony a few and takes more herself. They munch away, smiling at each other and wiping their mouths.)

PONY: *(Between swallows.)* How old are you?

OLIVIA: Eighty-one.

PONY: *Eighty-one...?* Gosh, that's so old!

OLIVIA: And how old are you?

PONY: Nine.

OLIVIA: *Nine...?* Is that all? I thought you were thirteen or fourteen...

PONY: No, just nine.

OLIVIA: I'm amazed!

PONY: When's your birthday?

OLIVIA: July 7th.

PONY: Oh, that's right. We just met a baby that was born on the same day. He was so cute. *(Pause.)* What's your favorite color?

OLIVIA: White. And yours?

PONY: Blue.

OLIVIA: Blue's all right.

PONY: And what's your favorite animal?

OLIVIA: The snowy owl. And yours?

PONY: *Horses!*

OLIVIA: Horses. Of course!

PONY: Do you have a lucky number?

OLIVIA: One.

PONY: *One?* That's so weird.

OLIVIA: What's yours?

PONY: Four.

OLIVIA: How come?

PONY: I don't know, it just is.

(Silence.)

OLIVIA: I like your glasses. Could I try them on?

PONY: Sure.

(She takes them off and hands them to her.)

OLIVIA: *(Putting them on.)* Ohhh, these are great! Everything's so clear! *(A silence as she gazes around the room.)*

PONY: How do you go to the bathroom if you have to stay in bed all day?

OLIVIA: In a bedpan.

PONY: What's that?

OLIVIA: A kind of portable toilet. Would you like to see it?

PONY: *(Thrilled.) Could I?!*

OLIVIA: Sure.

(She whips it out from under the covers and holds it aloft.)
What do you think?

PONY: Oh, that's neat!

OLIVIA: *(Handing it to her.)* Here, sit on it, it's like a little throne.

PONY: *(Puts it on the seat of her chair and sits on it.)*
Wow…! *(She makes a peeing sound.)* Pssssss…

OLIVIA: *(Offers her the first wig she had on.)* Now put this on for
the full effect…

PONY: *(Puts it on and tucks her hair inside.)* Psssss psssssss…

OLIVIA: *(Starts laughing and clapping her hands.)* Perfect, perfect!
(She suddenly has a seizure and grabs for the oxygen mask.)
Air…air…
(She gropes wildly to get it on.)
Help me, I can't get it on, I can't get it on…

PONY: *(Rises and gropes for the unit.)* Wait, I can't see…

OLIVIA: Air…air!

*(She finally gets it on. Her breathing becomes more labored. She
takes several more breaths and is restored. She removes the mask
and hangs it up. She gazes at Pony and smiles. A silence.)*

PONY: What happened?

(Olivia shuts her eyes and sighs.)
Are you OK?

OLIVIA: *(Drifting off to another world.)* Come, let's move into the
shade. I don't like all these bees.

BIG RIVER: The Adventures of Huckleberry Finn
(A Musical Play)
Book by William Hauptman Lyrics by Roger Miller
Adapted from the Novel by Mark Twain

The Characters: Jim (adult) and Huck (13-14)

This popular Broadway musical is a faithful and rousing retelling of
Mark Twain's great American classic, *The Adventures of Huckleberry
Finn*. Set along the Mississippi River Valley in the 1840s, young Huck
escapes his Pap and the Widow Douglas and all of the other
restrictions of civilization with his companion Jim, a runaway slave.
They set off down the great Mississippi on a raft, and along the way
encounter some of the most colorful characters in American literature,
including those oily conmen the Duke and the King. After a
considerable journey, Huck decides to head out to the western
territories before Tom Sawyer's Aunt Sally has a chance to adopt him
and tame him once and for all.

In the first scene below, Huck has just set off on his own when he
comes face to face with Jim.

HUCK: Hello, Jim!

JIM: Get back in the river where you belong, and don't do nothing to
ole Jim, who was always your friend!

HUCK: Jim, I'm not dead! I'm alive – and ever so glad to see you!

JIM: You ain't a ghost, is you?

HUCK: Touch me – I'm solid enough. I had to run away from Pap.
He got the *delirium tremens* and tried to stab me with his Barlow-
Knife. So I faked the whole thing.
(Jim just keeps staring. Huck addresses the audience.)
I talked along, but Jim just stood there. Finally he says –

JIM: See those birds flyin' low? That means rain. Let's go to my
camp.

HUCK: I followed Jim to a lean-to he'd built on the Illinois side.
*(A flash of lightning and a roll of thunder. They cross to a lean-to
An enormous catfish hangs from a line. There is a trunk and a raft
of logs nearby.)*

You got a great place here, Jim! That must be the biggest catfish ever pulled out of the Mississippi River!

JIM: *(Taking out knife and cutting down the fish.)* Found him on my trotline this morning. I was just getting ready to clean him up.

HUCK: I never seen a bigger one...what's all this?

JIM: Trash come floating down on the high water.

HUCK: *(Opening the trunk.)* Here's a calico gown...and some seegars...there must be a flood somewheres upriver...and look at this raft!

JIM: That came floating down, too.

HUCK: Jim? What *are* you doing here?

JIM: You wouldn't tell on me if I was to tell you?

HUCK: Blamed if I would, Jim.

JIM: Huck – I run off.

HUCK: Jim!

JIM: You said you wouldn't tell.

HUCK: And I'll stick to it, Jim, honest Injun. People can call me a dirty abolitionist and despise me for it – that don't make no difference. I ain't a-going to tell and I ain't a-going back there anyways – so let's hear about it.

JIM: Miss Watson always say she won't sell me. But I notice lately there's been a slave trader around the place considerable. The night you was killed, I creep to the door, and I hear the missus telling the Widow Douglas she's going to sell me down to New Orleans. She don't want to, but she can get eight hundred dollars for me, and it's such a big stack of money, she can't refuse. I never hear the rest. I light out.

(He cuts open the belly of the catfish – bloodlessly – and several objects spill out.)

Big fish like this eat all sorts of trash in his years.

HUCK: I'll say. Here's a spool.

JIM: And a horseshoe.

HUCK: *(Picks up a hard little sphere.)* What's this?

JIM: Must a been in there a long time to coat it over so.

(Jim cuts open the sphere and hands Huck a coin.)

HUCK: It's gold.

JIM: What sort of writing is that on it?

HUCK: Spanish...I think. This is a Spanish d'bloon, Jim, it's pirate gold! Why I reckon this fish could be a hundred years old. Do you reckon so, Jim?

JIM: *(Nodding.)* He go along on the bottom. Eat the little ones. Get older and older and bigger and bigger. He here before people come maybe. Before this was a country. When there was nothing here but that big river...

(He grabs Huck's arm.)

I'm going down that river, Huck. To Cairo, where the Mississippi joins the Ohio. Then I'm following the Ohio north, to the Free States. I'm going down on that raft, and I'm getting my freedom!

HUCK: I'm going with you, Jim!

JIM: You get in a powerful lot of trouble, helping Jim. You might find yourself hangin' from a cottonwood tree.

HUCK: You can't do it alone. But if I come along, I can tell people you belong to me, and they won't bother you.

JIM: *(Greatly moved.)* You'd do that for Jim? Then you a friend, Huck.

Here Jim and Huck have just begun their trip down the Mississippi.

(Huck and Jim, floating on the raft in the moonlight.)

HUCK: We'll travel by night. Eight nights should fetch us down to Cairo, where the Mississippi joins the Ohio. Then we'll sell this raft, maybe, and catch a steamboat north, to the Free States. Think we're going to make it?

JIM: Give me your left hand.

HUCK: You know all the signs, do you, Jim?

JIM: I know most every one there is.

HUCK: What do you see?

JIM: *(Examining his hand.)* Considerable trouble and considerable joy.

HUCK: That ain't much help. But we're a-going to make it, Jim – we got luck.

JIM: So long as we don't do nothing foolish.

HUCK: You mean like looking at the new moon over your left shoulder?

JIM: That, or touching a snakeskin with your bare hands.

HUCK: Looking at the new moon's the worst. Ole Hank Bunker did it, and bragged about it. And not two years later he got drunk and fell off the water tower, and spread himself out so he was just a

kind of layer, as you may say, and they had to slide him between
two doors for a coffin.

JIM: Look sharp. There's something up ahead.

HUCK: *(To audience.)* The river was still in flood, and all sorts of
things had come floating down on it.

*(They drift past ghostly sights, half seen in the almost total
darkness.)*

Look. There's a house, Jim, all tilted over like. And a steamboat
killed herself on a rock.

JIM: And a dead body.

*(A corpse floats in the river alongside the raft. Jim looks at it
closely.)*

He's drowned…I reckon he's only been dead a few hours.

HUCK: *(Eagerly.)* I never saw a dead body before!

JIM: *(With strange intensity.)* No, Huck! Don't look at his face – it's
too ghastly! Let him go on his way.

(He releases the corpse. The river carries it out of sight.)

HUCK: What's wrong with you, Jim?

JIM: Don't talk no more 'bout it.

HUCK: Why wouldn't you let me look at him?

JIM: You want him to come back and haunt us? A man who's not
buried is more likely to go a-haunting than one who's planted and
comfortable.

HUCK: *(To audience.)* That sounded pretty reasonable, so I didn't
say no more.

JIM: Here's daylight.

HUCK: *(To audience.)* When the sun rose, we tied up the raft where
nobody could see it and slept; and later I told Jim stories about the
great kings of the world.

*(Huck and Jim are lying on the raft in the green shade of the river
bank. Pencils of sunlight fall through the leaves. The cicadas
drone.)*

JIM: I never knowed there was so many kings. Onliest one I ever
heard of was King Solomon – 'less you count the kings on a deck
of cards. Ain't no kings in America, is there, Huck?

HUCK: Some say King Louis the Fourteen of France had a little boy,
the Dolphin, who came over here to America when his pa got his
head chopped off.

JIM: But if there ain't no kings here, he'd be lonely. What would he
do? He couldn't get no situation.

HUCK: Join the police force, maybe. Or teach people how to speak French.

JIM: Why don't the French people speak the way we do?

HUCK: Jim, you couldn't understand a word of it.

(Sitting up.)

Suppose someone was to come up to you and say *polly voo franzy,* what would you think?

JIM: I wouldn't think nothing; I'd take an' bust him in the head – that is, if he weren't white.

HUCK: It ain't calling you anything. It's just saying do you know how to speak French.

JIM: Well then, why don't he just *say* it?

HUCK: He *is* saying it; that's the French way of saying it.

JIM: Well, it's a blame ridiculous way of saying it, and I don't want to hear no more about it.

HUCK: I give up, Jim; it's impossible to learn you anything.

JIM: How much do a king get, Huck?

HUCK: As much as he wants; everything belongs to him. Why, he could get – a thousand dollars a day.

JIM: Ain't *that* gay? And what he got to do to get it?

HUCK: Nothing.

JIM: Nothing?

HUCK: Nothing.

JIM: You mean he just lays around, like we're doing?

HUCK: 'Cept when things is dull. Then he fusses with the Parliament. And if everybody doesn't go just so, he chops their heads off.

JIM: *(Rising.)* Then I reckon we're just as well off as kings.

HUCK: 'Cept we ain't rich.

JIM: Well, I got more money now than I ever had. I owns myself – and I'm worth eight hundred dollars. Come on, let's fix something to eat.

HUCK: *(To audience.)* Then we'd have catfish and cornbread, or sometimes, I lifted a chicken from a farmer and took her along. Pap always said, take a chicken when you get the chance, because if you don't want it, you can easy find somebody that does, and a good deed ain't never forgot. I never seen Pap when he didn't want the chicken himself, but that's what he used to say anyway. When it got dark, we'd shove off.

(Now they are on the river again. The moon is waning, and sheds

less light.)

JIM: Light that lantern, Huck. We don't want to get run down.
(Huck lights the lantern hanging from a stick on the bow. His face can be seen in its orange glow.)

HUCK: Sometimes I'd catch myself thinking about that dead man.

JIM: Forget it, Huck. It'll bring bad luck.

HUCK: But I couldn't keep from studying over it, wondering who he was.

JIM: Look yonder!
(Spread across the horizon are the lights of St. Louis.)

HUCK: The fifth night, we floated past St. Louis.

JIM: What a wonderful spread of lights.

HUCK: They say there's twenty or thirty thousand people living in St. Louis, but I never believed it till now.

JIM: Lord, it looks like the whole world lit up.

HUCK: And not a sound; everybody must be asleep.

JIM: Three more nights should fetch us to Cairo!
(Singing is heard in the distance.)

HUCK: Listen! What's that?
(A flatboat appears, rowed along by a crew of slaves in chains who sing as they row. In the stern is a white overseer with a shotgun.)

JIM: Slaves who tried to run off, like me. But they got caught. Now they crossing back.

HUCK: How do you figure that?

JIM: I hears it in their singing.

The Characters: Huck (13-14) and Tom (10-12)

In this scene Huck has come to the cabin of Tom Sawyer's Uncle Phelps, who has captured Jim and is holding him in a shed. Huck is pretending to be Tom, whom the Phelps's haven't seen in a long while, when in comes the real Tom for a visit.

(Huck, crossing the stage, encounters Tom Sawyer carrying a small suitcase.)

HUCK: *(To audience.)* Sure enough, before long I seen him coming. *(To Tom:)* Hold on!

TOM: *(Unable to believe his eyes.)* What do you want to come back and haunt me for? I never done you no harm!

HUCK: I ain't come back – I never been gone.

TOM: Honest Injun, you ain't a ghost?

HUCK: Honest Injun.

TOM: But look here: weren't you ever murdered at all?

HUCK: Not at all. I played it on 'em. Come here and feel if you don't believe me.

TOM: *(Does.)* What have you been doing with yourself?

HUCK: Having a grand, mysterious adventure that I ain't got time to tell you about right now.

TOM: I'm visiting my aunt, Sally Phelps.

HUCK: I know. I'm there right now – playing *you* Now listen. Your Uncle Silas has got Jim locked in his shed.

TOM: Ole Miss Watson's Jim?

HUCK: He's been traveling along with me. Here's the important thing, Tom. I'm going to steal Jim out of slavery!

TOM: But you don't need –

HUCK: I know what you'll say. It's a dirty, low-down business, but what if it is? I'm low-down too, and I'm going to steal him, and you won't let on, will you?

TOM: *(Gleefully.)* I'll *help* you steal him.

HUCK: You're joking.

TOM: I ain't joking.

HUCK: I'm bound to say, you just fell considerable in my estimation. Tom Sawyer a dirty abolitionist? I can't believe it.

TOM: Well, I'm a-going to do it. Didn't I say I was going to?

HUCK: Yes.

TOM: *Well,* then.

HUCK: All right, here's my plan: I fetch my raft.

TOM: *(Nodding.)* Raft.

HUCK: Then, first dark night, I steal the key to the shed from your uncle's britches.

TOM: *(Nodding.)* Britches.

HUCK: We release Jim, then shove off downriver. Won't that work?

TOM: Work? Certainly, but it's too simple. What's the good of a plan that ain't no more trouble than that? It's mild as goose milk. Let me think.

HUCK: *(To audience.)* So he thought.

TOM: We'll dig him out.

HUCK: Dig?

TOM: With spoons. It should take about a week. As things stand, it's just too simple. That's what makes it so rotten difficult to come up with a difficult plan. I bet there ain't even a watchdog to give sleeping mixture to. I bet there ain't even a moat. If we get time, the night of the escape we might dig one. How's that sound?

HUCK: *(To audience.)* I seen Tom's plan was worth fifteen of mine for style. It would make Jim just as free, and might get us both killed besides. *(To Tom.)* I'm satisfied.

TOM: Bully! Let's go look at that shed.

THE CHILDREN'S HOUR
by Lillian Hellman

The Characters: Evelyn (12-14), Mary (12-14) and Peggy (12-14)

Karen Wright and Martha Dobie run a boarding school for girls. All seems well until one of the students, Mary Tilford, begins to spread malicious rumors about Karen and Martha's relationship. Before the truth can be told, the accusations damage the school, destroy Karen's marriage plans, and lead to Martha's suicide.

In the scene that follows, a vengeful Mary has dispatched Rosalie to move Mary's things, hinting at a secret she would disclose about Rosalie if she refuses. intimidated by Mary's strength, and fearful of having Peggy and Evelyn hear her secret, she has reluctantly agreed and exited.

EVELYN: Now what do you think of that? What made her so agreeable?

MARY: *(Closes door, crosses downstage, sits in chair right of desk.)* Oh, a little secret we got. Go on, now, what else did she say?

PEGGY: Well, Mortar said that Dobie was jealous of them, and that she was like that when she was a little girl, and that she'd better get herself a beau of her own because it was unnatural, and that she never wanted anybody to like Miss Wright, and that was unnatural. Boy! Did Miss Dobie get sore at that!

EVELYN: Then we didn't hear any more. Peggy dropped some books.

MARY: What'd she mean Dobie was jealous?

PEGGY: What's unnatural.

EVELYN: Un for not. Not natural.

PEGGY: It's funny, because everybody gets married.

MARY: A lot of people don't – they're too ugly.

PEGGY: *(Claps hand to her mouth.)* Oh, my God! Rosalie'll find that copy of *Mademoiselle de Maupin.* She'll blab like the dickens.

MARY: Ah, she won't say a word.

EVELYN: *(Leans toward Mary.)* Who gets the book when we move?

MARY: You can have it. That's what I was doing this morning –
finishing it. There's one part in it –

PEGGY: What part?

(Mary laughs.)

EVELYN: Well, what was it?

MARY: Wait until you read it.

EVELYN: Did you understand it? I don't always –

PEGGY: It's a shame about being moved. I don't want to go in with
Helen: she's John's cousin, you know, and I don't want to talk
about the whole thing.

EVELYN: What whole thing? You've only met him once.

MARY: It was a dirty trick making us move. She just wants to see
how much fun she can take away from me. She hates me.

PEGGY: No, she doesn't, Mary. She treats you just like the rest of
us – almost better.

MARY: That's right, stick up for your crush. Take her side against
mine.

PEGGY: I didn't mean it that way.

EVELYN: *(Looks at her watch. Rises.)* We'd better get upstairs.

MARY: I'm not going.

PEGGY: Rosalie isn't so bad.

EVELYN: What you going to do about the kitten?

MARY: I don't care about Rosalie and I don't care about the kitten.
*(Mary grabs what is left of kitten. Peggy and Evelyn take it away
from her.)* I'm not going to be here.

PEGGY: Not going to be here!

EVELYN: What do you mean?

MARY: *(Calmly.)* I'm going home.

PEGGY: Oh, Mary –

EVELYN: You can't do that.

MARY: Oh, can't I? You just watch. I'm not staying here.
*(Rises, slowly crosses left below desk to upper left of chair left of
desk.)* I'm going home and tell Grandma I'm not staying any
more. *(Smiles to herself.)* I'll tell her I'm not happy. They're
scared of Grandma – she helped 'em when they first started, you
know – and when she tells 'em something, believe me, they'll sit
up and listen. They can't get away with treating me like this, and
they don't have to think they can.

PEGGY: *(Appalled.)* You just going to walk out like that?

EVELYN: What you going to tell your grandmother?

MARY: Oh, who cares? I'll think of something to tell her. I can always do it better on the spur of the moment.

PEGGY: *(Rises.)* She'll send you right back.

MARY: *(Crosses to down left table, fingers lamp.)* You let me worry about that. Grandma's very fond of me, on account my father was her favorite son. My father killed himself, but Grandma won't admit it. I can manage *her* all right.

PEGGY: I don't think you ought to go, really, Mary. It's just going to make an awful lot of noise.

EVELYN: What's going to happen about the kitten?

MARY: Say I did it – it doesn't make a bit of difference any more to me. *(Crosses back to upper left of chair, left of desk.)* Now listen, you two got to help. They won't miss me before dinner if you make Rosalie shut the door and keep it shut. Now, I'll go through the field to French's, and then I can get the bus to Homestead.

EVELYN: How you going to get to the street car?

MARY: Taxi, idiot.

PEGGY: How are you going to get out of here in the first place?

MARY: *(Slowly moving downstage.)* I'm going to walk out. I know where they keep the front door. Well, I'm going right out the door.

EVELYN: Gee, I wouldn't have the nerve.

MARY: Of course you wouldn't. You'd let 'em do anything to you they want. Well, they can't do it to me. *(Turns to them.)* Who's got any money?
(Peggy slowly crosses right above desk, comes downstage between sofa and desk to below left end of sofa.)

EVELYN: *(Moves to above chair right of desk.)* Not me. Not a cent. Not a cent.

MARY: I've got to have a dollar for the taxi and a dime for the bus.

EVELYN: And where you going to find it?

PEGGY: *(Below left end of sofa.)* See? Why don't you just wait until you get your allowance on Monday, and then you can go any place you want. Maybe by that time –

MARY: I'm going today. *Now.*

EVELYN: You can't walk to Laneet.

MARY: *(Slowly crosses right below desk to center. To Peggy.)* You've got money. You've got three dollars and twenty-five cents. Go get it for me.

PEGGY: *(Moves away right below sofa.)* No! No! I won't get it for you.

EVELYN: *(Crosses to center.)* You can't have that money, Mary –

MARY: *(Advances to below left end of sofa.)* Get it for me.

PEGGY: *(Cringes, her voice is scared.)* I won't. I just won't.
Mamma doesn't send me much allowance – not half as much as
the rest of you get – I saved this so long – you took it from me
last time –

EVELYN: *(Comes down left of Mary.)* Ah, she wants that dress so
bad.

PEGGY: I'll tell you a secret. I'd never even go to the movies if
Miss Wright and Miss Dobie didn't give me money. I never have
anything the rest of you get all the time. It took me so long to save
that and I –

MARY: Go upstairs and get me the money.

PEGGY: *(Hysterically, backing away from her.)* I won't. I won't. I
won't.
*(Mary makes a sudden move to her, grabs her arm, and jerks it
back, hard and expertly. Peggy screams softly. Evelyn tries to take
Mary's arm away. Without releasing her hold on Peggy, Mary
slaps Evelyn's face. Evelyn backs away, begins to cry.)*

MARY: Just say when you've had enough.

PEGGY: *(Softly, stiflingly.)* All – all right – I'll get it.

MARY: *(Smiles, nods her head, releases Peggy, softly.)* Go on, go on.
*(Peggy, crying and rubbing her arm, slowly crosses toward door
as curtain falls.)*

CHOOSING SIDES FOR BASKETBALL
by Kathryn Schultz Miller

The Characters: Danny (9), Reggie (9), Melinda (9) and Georgie (9)

Miller's play tells the stories of four children who are waiting to be chosen for a basketball team at school. Dan discovers that having a little sister isn't so bad after all. Reggie can't understand how Dad can still love him after giving him a spanking. Melinda suffers a terrible nightmare in which she confronts a horrifying monster – her babysitter. And the new kid in school, little Georgie, is finally chosen to play even though she wears glasses. The scene below opens the play.

(Danny and Melinda will enter from one side and Georgie and Reggie will enter from the other. Danny blows the whistle and all come running down the aisles, calling to each other, as if they are playing before gym class begins.)

DANNY: Hi ya, Reggie!

REGGIE: *(Calling from across the room, as he enters playing area.)* Hey, Danny, throw me the ball!
(Both arrive on stage and throw the ball back and forth to each other. They have just been let out of class and are full of energy.)

MELINDA: Hey, you guys, I want to play too! Over here. Reggie, throw it to me!
(They start to play. The boys are not altogether happy to have Melinda join them. Georgie has entered slightly behind the rest and has taken her place on the center cube. She is doing simple exercises, sometimes taking notice of the others around her. She is trying hard to look occupied even though she feels left out. Others continue to play until Reggie begins showing off doing tricks with the ball.)

DANNY: *(Taking the ball away from Reggie.)* Hey, look what I can do. My cousin taught me. *(He tries to balance the ball on his forefinger but it keeps falling off.)* Don't laugh. I'll get it, just wait a minute.

REGGIE: *(Taking the ball away from Danny, acting cocky.)* Danny, I don't know why you even bother. Here let me show you how. *(He balances the ball perfectly on his finger.)*

MELINDA: Oh, Reggie, you're always showing off.

REGGIE: See, Danny, now that's how it's done. *(Still balancing ball.)*

DANNY: *(His pride is hurt.)* Why do you act so smart, Reggie? You *failed* gym class last report card.

REGGIE: *(Embarrassed.)* So what. *(He bounces the ball hard in Danny's direction and walks away.)*

MELINDA: *(Taking ball from Danny.)* Come on, guys, let me try.

REGGIE: *(Noticing Georgie.)* Hey, why don't you play, Georgie?

MELINDA: *(Taunting.)* Oh, she won't play. *(Walking over to Reggie and giggling.)* Georgie, Porgie, puddin' an' pie! *(She and Reggie laugh.)*

DANNY: *(Noticing Georgie's discomfort.)* Cut it out, Melinda. Hey, Reggie, let's play keep away from Melinda.
(They throw the ball back and forth, over Melinda's head so that she can't reach it. They are calling "Keep away, Keep away, Keep away." The boys are laughing and Melinda is running back and forth, getting out of breath.)

MELINDA: You guys! Come on! I don't like this! Quit!
(Georgie watches as they play keep away. Finally Melinda makes a jump for it, looses her balance and falls into Danny. They both fall to the ground. Melinda laughs out loud because she has stopped their taunting. While on the ground Danny blows the whistle; the audience should not see him do this.)

MELINDA: I told you class was going to start. Get in line!
(Georgie puts the cube upstage next to the banner and runs to her place in line, on top of the ladder. The others are lined up on the sides of her, looking out into the distance.)

REGGIE: I hate it when they make us choose sides for basketball.

MELINDA: Who is it this time?
(All look to see who has been designated "captain." All actors' eyes focus on one place, some squint.)

GEORGIE: *(To Danny.)* Who are the captains?

DANNY: He's new. He's from the 6th grade class. He's so bad they held him back a year. But he sure is good at basketball. He must be seven feet tall.

REGGIE: Now he's in our gym class.

MELINDA: His name is Benjamin Schwartz.

DANNY: But they call him "Benny Bingo." Because he always says "bingo" when he shoots a basket.

REGGIE: Yeah, and he does that a lot.

MELINDA: *(Pointing.)* And that's Allison Bronson. She's the other captain. Boy, she's tough, too.

GEORGIE: They'll never pick me. I'll be sitting here till the very last and they'll never pick me.

REGGIE: *(Crossing his fingers.)* I hope they pick me.

GEORGIE: I wish I were invisible.

REGGIE: I hope. I hope.

MELINDA: Oh, don't worry, Reggie, you're good. Benny Bingo will pick you for sure.

REGGIE: I failed gym class last report card.

MELINDA: How did you fail?

REGGIE: The teacher said I didn't concentrate enough, whatever that means.

MELINDA: What did your Mom and Dad say?

REGGIE: *(Walking out from his place in line.)* It wasn't very nice.

CONVICTS
by Horton Foote

The Characters: Horace (13) and Convict (adult)

Horace Robedaux is all alone. He doesn't have a place with his family. His father divorced his mother and has died, leaving no money and no home. Horace's mother and sister, Lily Dale, have moved to Houston to find a home and work, but there wasn't room for Horace. Horace is left to stay at a decrepit plantation, worked by the convicts from the neighboring prison. All that is really important to Horace right now is to make enough money to put a tombstone on his father's grave. In this scene, Horace has been left to watch over a chained convict who has attempted to run away.

*SPECIAL NOTE: You may wish to also read *The Death of Papa* and *Roots in a Parched Ground,* part of the series of plays about Horace Robedaux, also featured in this volume.

HORACE: *(Pause.)* My name is Horace. *(Pause.)* What's your name?
CONVICT: Leroy.
HORACE: Leroy what?
CONVICT: Leroy Kendricks.
HORACE: There are a lot of Kendricks out around Kendelton. Are you kin to them?
CONVICT: No.
HORACE: Everybody that lives there is colored.
CONVICT: I still never been there. I come from Louisiana.
HORACE: How did you get down here?
CONVICT: I was working in the cane fields over in Brazoria County and I got into a fight and I cut a man.
HORACE: What did you cut him for?
CONVICT: What do you mean, what I cut him for?
HORACE: Were you mad at him?
CONVICT: Sure, I was mad at him. I was drunk, but I was mad at him too.
HORACE: Did you cut him bad?

CONVICT: No. He hollered like I kilt him, but I only cut him across the face. Anyway, they sentenced me to the Retrieve Prison Plantation on the coast. That's the worst place I was ever in in my life. I heard you could hire out to work on plantations around here until you paid off your fine, so I asked if I could go work out my fine and they sent me here.

HORACE: What's your fine?

CONVICT: Five hundred dollars. They pay me seven dollars a month, or they pay the state for me to pay off my fine.

HORACE: How long have you been here?

CONVICT: About a year.

HORACE: Twelve months?

CONVICT: I think so. No, not quite – I'd say nearer ten months. Tomorrow is Christmas, isn't it?

HORACE: Yes.

CONVICT: It was quite a spell after Christmas. They were planting when I got here.

HORACE: How long will you have to work at seven dollars a month to pay off your fine?

CONVICT: I don't know. They didn't tell me.

HORACE: Didn't you figure it out?

CONVICT: How am I going to figure it out?

HORACE: Just figure it out.

CONVICT: I don't know how.

HORACE: Did you go to school?

CONVICT: No.

HORACE: Never?

CONVICT: No.

HORACE: I went to the sixth grade, then I came out here to work with my uncle. Let's see – seven dollars a month at twelve months is eighty-four dollars. Eighty-four dollars into five hundred is ... *(Pause.)* I can't do that in my head. I'll have to go back to the store and get a pencil to do that. I get four bits a week. Plus my room and board. I know how much I'll earn after I been here a year – twenty-four dollars. Of course, I ain't seen any of it yet. I go to Mr. Soll every other day and ask him to pay me and he always says he'll pay me tomorrow. But tomorrow never comes. *(Pause.)* You got any folks?

CONVICT: Sure.

HORACE: Where?

CONVICT: I don't know now. Used to be around New Iberia, Louisiana, last I heard.

HORACE: Do they know where you are?

CONVICT: No.

HORACE: Didn't you get word to them?

CONVICT: How am I going to do that? I can't write and they can't read.

HORACE: I been doing some figuring in my head. It comes to almost six years to pay off five hundred dollars.

CONVICT: It's going to be more than that now…*(Pause.)* because I kilt a man now.

HORACE: How come you kilt him?

CONVICT: Because he was always bothering me.

HORACE: How was he bothering you?

CONVICT: Just like I say. I told him to stop and he wouldn't. I told him if he didn't stop I was going to kill him first chance I got. I reckon he knew I meant what I said now.

HORACE: What was his name?

CONVICT: Jessie.

HORACE: Jessie what?

CONVICT: Jessie Wilkes.

HORACE: How old was he?

CONVICT: He was young.

HORACE: How old?

CONVICT: Twenty-two or so, I reckon. He has a brother here too. Brother says he gonna kill me if the white sheriff don't kill me.

HORACE: You scared of him?

CONVICT: No. His name is Sherman. Sherman Edwards.

HORACE: How come they are brothers if one is named Wilkes and one's named Edwards?

CONVICT: They had the same mama but a different daddy. He had a white man for a daddy.

HORACE: Who did?

CONVICT: Sherman Edwards. That's why he's so mean. It's the white blood in him. He'd kill you too, if he got a chance…mean as he is. He don't like white people. He says he'd kill them all if he got the chance. "How come you don't like white people," I asked him, "when you're half white?" He didn't answer that. He just cussed me. *(Pause.)* After I killed Jessie, I thought I might run for the brush and try to get away, but they're devils around here and they'd catch you sooner or later. I heard they caught one colored man who was a convict and stealing cattle to keep alive. And they caught him as he was butchering one of the cows he stole, and they grabbed him and sewed him up alive in the carcass of that cow as an example to all the cattle thieves.

HORACE: What do you think happened to him?

CONVICT: I think he died. That's what I think happened to him. *(Pause.)* If you give me that knife I might just cut my own throat and save somebody else the trouble. *(Pause.)* Would you give me the knife?

HORACE: No.

CONVICT: Would you give me another chew of tobacco?

HORACE: Sure. *(He chucks it to him.)* Keep it.
(The Convict tears off a piece and begins to chew. He puts the rest in his pocket.)

CONVICT: Overseer say they going to take me to the county jail. What's the name of the town that's at?

HORACE: Harrison. That's where I come from.

CONVICT: You born there?

HORACE: Yes.

CONVICT: You got people there?

HORACE: I told you – an uncle and some aunts.

CONVICT: You didn't tell me nothing.

HORACE: I thought I did. My daddy is dead. My mama and my baby sister live in Houston.

CONVICT: How come you're not with your mama?

HORACE: She lives in a small house. She's got no room for me. How did you get to Texas from New Iberia?

CONVICT: I ran away.

HORACE: I ran away too, once. Did I tell you that?

CONVICT: Yes, you did.

HORACE: I could run forever now and nobody would even know I was gone.

CONVICT: If you were running away from here, which way would you go?

HORACE: Depends on where I was running to. If you want to get to Houston, it's one way –

CONVICT: How far is Houston?

HORACE: Sixty miles. That's where my mama lives. Did I tell you that?

CONVICT: Yes, you did.

HORACE: Galveston is ninety. Corpus Christi is ninety. The gulf is thirty-five.

CONVICT: All in the same direction?

HORACE: No.

CONVICT: If you was heading for Corpus, how would you go?

HORACE: I never been there, but I would head for the river and follow that to the gulf and then head south.

CONVICT: How far is the river?

HORACE: About a quarter of a mile.

CONVICT: Which direction?

HORACE: *(Pointing.)* That way. Can you swim?

CONVICT: A little bit.

HORACE: Stay away from the river if you can't swim. There are alligators and suckholes down there. People are always drowning in the river. I'm a good swimmer.

CONVICT: How did you learn?

HORACE: I taught myself. I was raised by the river. I'm going to ask Mr. Soll for my money I've earned so far when he gets back from Harrison today. It's Christmas Eve, so I figure he'll be in a good humor and he'll give it to me. Did I tell you what I was gonna do with my money?

CONVICT: Yes, you did.

HORACE: I don't know how big a tombstone I can get for twenty-four dollars, but I guess I can get some kind. If I give you this knife, would you really try to kill yourself?

CONVICT: Give it to me and see.

HORACE: I couldn't do that.

CONVICT: You're not in chains waitin' for a sheriff.

HORACE: I couldn't do it. I'm afraid of dying. You're not afraid of dying?

CONVICT: No.

(Horace starts away.)

CONVICT: Where are you going?

HORACE: I'm going to say a prayer over Jessie's grave. *(Pause.)* Is it Jessie or Sherman?

CONVICT: Jessie. Why are you doing that?

HORACE: Because I feel bad he was dumped into the ground and no prayer was said.

CONVICT: How come you feel bad about it? You didn't know him.

HORACE: I just do. Did you ever go to a funeral?

CONVICT: No.

HORACE: Neither have I. So I don't know what they do. When my daddy was buried I didn't get to go to his funeral because they said I was too young; and Mr. John Howard's wife took his body back to Waxahachie because she hated Harrison and all its people, she said; and Mr. Ritter wandered off into the woods one winter day and they never have found his body, only his gun, and some people think he's still alive. Excuse me, I'm just going over there and say the Lord's Prayer.

(He goes off. The Convict lies down on the ground again and closes his eyes. Horace comes back in.)

Do you know the Lord's Prayer?

CONVICT: No.

THE DEATH OF PAPA
by Horton Foote

The Characters: Horace, Jr. (12) and Gertrude (adult)

Horace, Jr., comes home at the beginning of the play to hear the news
that his grandfather, Henry Vaughn, has died. Mr. Vaughn has headed
the family for many years and everyone is naturally upset. Times of
passing are times of change. The adults that Horace, Jr., deals with (his
mother and father, a black house staff, Gertrude, his wild, heavy-
drinking Uncle Brother Vaughn) all seem on the edge. Horace, Jr., is
also extemely curious about everything: life, death, babies, money,
trying to sort out where his life will take him.
   In the first scene, Horace, Jr., has a private opportunity to ask
Gertrude, his friend and confidant, about the differences between their
races.

*SPECIAL NOTE: You may wish to read *Convicts* and *Roots in a
Parched Ground,* part of the series of plays about Horace Robedaux
also featured in this volume.

(Gertrude picks up the book Horace, Jr., is reading.)
GERTRUDE: *The Adventures of Huckleberry Finn.*
HORACE, JR.: Did you ever read that?
GERTRUDE: No.
HORACE, JR.: Did you ever read *The Adventures of Tom Sawyer.*
GERTRUDE: No.
HORACE, JR.: What books have you read?
GERTRUDE: I don't know. Not many.
HORACE, JR.: Don't you read books in your school?
GERTRUDE: No.
HORACE, JR.: Then how come you go to school?
GERTRUDE: To learn things.
HORACE, JR.: What?
GERTRUDE: To be a nurse or a teacher.
HORACE, JR.: What do you want to be that for?
GERTRUDE: To help my people.
HORACE, JR.: Who are your people? Your mama and daddy?

GERTRUDE: No. My people...my race. That's what Professor McCann says we're in school for. To help our race. Isn't that what you go to school for?

HORACE, JR.: I don't know. I never heard about it, if I did.

GERTRUDE: Professor McCann is as light as you are.

HORACE, JR.: Is he white?

GERTRUDE: No. He's just light. He has a son studying to be a doctor. He buys all his clothes at your daddy's store. I see him in there buying clothes almost every Saturday when I go uptown. My mama bought a shirt last Saturday at your daddy's store. She says he's a good friend to all the colored people around here. She says they all like him. So was your granddaddy. My mama went to his funeral this afternoon. I sure wanted to go, but she said I could do more good by coming over here and helping out. "But I don't want to spend my life nursing children, Mama, the way you have," I said. "No indeed. I want to be a nurse for the sick or a schoolteacher. I'm going to college."

HORACE, JR.: Where are you going?

GERTRUDE: Prairie View Normal.

HORACE, JR.: That's the colored college.

GERTRUDE: Yes, it is. Are you going to college?

HORACE, JR.: I don't know. My daddy never went to college. His daddy did, though. He was a lawyer. *(He whispers.)* My daddy was twelve when his daddy died. His mama and daddy were separated. He doesn't know I know that, but I heard him and Mama talking one night. He doesn't like the man my grandmama is married to now.

GERTRUDE: Why?

HORACE, JR.: Because he was mean to him when he was a boy. He said if his daddy had lived, his whole life would have been different. Do you think so?

GERTRUDE: I wouldn't know.

HORACE, JR.: You got a grandfather?

GERTRUDE: No. And I don't have a daddy, neither. Your grandfather that just died was a smart man. Did he go to college?

HORACE, JR.: Sure. He went to A & M. He graduated with honors. I had another grandfather, too. He died at thirty-two. A drunkard. He went to college, though. He was a lawyer. What were your grandfathers like?

GERTRUDE: I don't know anything about them.

HORACE, JR.: I know about my daddy's grandfather on his mother's side. And his great-grandfather, he was acting governor of Texas during the war with Mexico. He had two big plantations with one hundred twenty slaves.

GERTRUDE: I'm glad I didn't live then.

HORACE, JR.: Why?

GERTRUDE: Because I wouldn't want to be a slave. Would you?

HORACE, JR.: No. Would you have been a slave?

GERTRUDE: Yes.

HORACE, JR.: Why?

GERTRUDE: Because colored people were the slaves. But no more. And you're not going to do to us what you did to the Indians.

HORACE, JR.: What did we do to the Indians?

GERTRUDE: Killed them all off and moved them onto reservations.

The Characters: Horace, Jr. (12) and Elizabeth (adult)

In this scene Horace, Jr., tries to get some important questions answered by his mother, Elizabeth.

HORACE, JR.: Why does Daddy need money?

ELIZABETH: He just does.

HORACE, JR.: I heard him say the other night he had been worried about money all his life. Why is that?

ELIZABETH: He's just worried is all.

HORACE, JR.: Do we have enough to eat?

ELIZABETH: Yes, we do. Now, you know we do.

HORACE, JR.: Do you think he will lose his store?

ELIZABETH: Why would you think that?

HORACE, JR.: I heard him talking to you. He said he owed the bank so much money he was afraid they wouldn't loan him any more and he'd lose everything.

ELIZABETH: Don't you ever repeat that to anyone. Do you hear me?

HORACE, JR.: Daddy works hard.

ELIZABETH: Yes, he does.

HORACE, JR.: Aren't you supposed to have money when you work hard?

ELIZABETH: I think you are.

HORACE, JR.: Why doesn't he?

ELIZABETH: I don't know. His business depends on the cotton crop and the cotton crop hasn't done well lately.

HORACE, JR.: Does everybody around here depend upon the cotton crop?

ELIZABETH: More or less.

HORACE, JR.: Is everybody poor?

ELIZABETH: No, I can't say that.

HORACE, JR.: Why is that?

ELIZABETH: I can't explain it; it's just how things are.

HORACE, JR.: Does everybody owe money at the bank?

ELIZABETH: No.

HORACE, JR.: Is Grandma poor?

ELIZABETH: No, you know she's not.

HORACE, JR.: Is she rich?

ELIZABETH: In a way.

HORACE, JR.: Is she the richest person here?

ELIZABETH: Oh, no. Not by any means.

HORACE, JR.: Is Gertrude poor?

ELIZABETH: Yes.

HORACE, JR.: Why?

ELIZABETH: Because she hasn't any money.

HORACE, JR.: Does her mother have money?

ELIZABETH: No.

HORACE, JR.: Why?

ELIZABETH: Because she doesn't get paid much.

HORACE, JR.: She works hard?

ELIZABETH: Yes.

HORACE, JR.: Why doesn't she get paid, then?

ELIZABETH: Because that's how things are.

HORACE, JR.: Did you ever work?

ELIZABETH: Yes. I taught piano.

HORACE, JR.: Did you get paid very much?

ELIZABETH: No. Not too much.

HORACE, JR.: Is Eliza Gertrude's mother?

ELIZABETH: No, her aunt. And Walter is her uncle.

HORACE, JR.: Gertrude said she would like to be a nurse or a teacher someday to help her race.

ELIZABETH: Did she?

HORACE, JR.: I'd like to help my race, too. What can I do?

ELIZABETH: Well, I don't know. We'll have to think about it. Start by being a good man; that will help all the races.

HORACE, JR.: How do I be a good man?

ELIZABETH: God only knows, honey.

HORACE, JR.: Is Daddy a good man?

ELIZABETH: I think so. I know he tries to be.

HORACE, JR.: Was Papa?

ELIZABETH: Oh, yes. Very good!

HORACE, JR.: Why?

ELIZABETH: Because he was.

HORACE, JR.: Was Daddy's father...Mister Paul Horace?

ELIZABETH: Don't call him Mister, honey, he's your grandfather, too.

HORACE, JR.: What should I call him?

ELIZABETH: Grandfather.

HORACE, JR.: Will I ever see him?

ELIZABETH: I expect so, some day.

HORACE, JR.: When?

ELIZABETH: In heaven.

HORACE, JR.: He drank whiskey and smoked cigarettes. I don't think you get to heaven if you do that.

ELIZABETH: Who told you that?

HORACE, JR.: I heard Miss Ida say it. She said God wouldn't have you if you did that.

ELIZABETH: Who did she say that to?

HORACE, JR.: Her boy.

ELIZABETH: Well, I don't believe that.

HORACE, JR.: You mean I can smoke and drink and still go to heaven?

ELIZABETH: Oh, honey, I don't know really what gets us to heaven or keeps us away.

HORACE, JR.: Uncle Brother drinks and smokes.

ELIZABETH: I know.

HORACE, JR.: Is he going to heaven?

ELIZABETH: I hope so.

HORACE, JR.: If I see Daddy's papa in heaven, how am I going to know him? I have never seen a picture of him.

ELIZABETH: Oh, I don't know, honey.

HORACE, JR.: How will he know me? He's never seen a picture of me either.

ELIZABETH: What?

HORACE, JR.: I said...*(Pause.)* You aren't half listening to me.

ELIZABETH: Yes, I am.

HORACE, JR.: Are you worried?

ELIZABETH: No.

HORACE, JR.: Where's Henry Vaughn?

ELIZABETH: He's out riding with your grandfather. They went out to the farms. *(Pause.)* Son, Mother is going to have another baby.

HORACE, JR.: Are you? When?

ELIZABETH: In six months.

HORACE, JR.: Is it going to be a boy or a girl?

ELIZABETH: I don't know. You can't ever know that.

HORACE, JR.: What do you want?

ELIZABETH: I'd like a girl, since I have two boys.

HORACE, JR.: You have a girl, too. She is dead, but you have her. What happens to you when you die?

ELIZABETH: I don't know.

HORACE, JR.: Do you change?

ELIZABETH: Honey, I just don't know.

HORACE, JR.: Suppose I die...

ELIZABETH: You're not going to die.

HORACE, JR.: Why? Could you keep me from it?

EAST OF THE SUN AND WEST OF THE MOON
Adapted by Claudia Ferguson
From the Short Story by Asbjornsen and Moe

The Characters: Coby (ageless) and Waldo (ageless)

In this fairy tale Helga, Queen of the Trolls, turns the handsome Prince, Justin, into a ferocious white bear. When she sends two of her trolls to capture the Prince, her magic is thwarted by the lovely girl Lara, who is in love with the White Bear/Prince. In the end, Lara saves Justin with the aid of the Mother of the Winds.

In the first scene below, the trolls Coby and Waldo have just met the beautiful and sweet-tempered Lara.

COBY: Why do you keep calling her pretty lady? I thought you hated mortal people.

WALDO: A troll has to be two-faced.

COBY: I forgot.

WALDO: We pretend to be friendly.

COBY: She is very pretty.

WALDO: Stupid! Do you think that matters?

COBY: I sort of like her.

WALDO: A troll never likes a mortal person. Keep that in mind.

COBY: Yes, Waldo.

WALDO: The White Bear is coming here and we have to find out why.

COBY: I'm getting tired of following him around.

WALDO: Do you want to be a Tenderfoot Troll forever?

COBY: Oh, no, I want to learn.

WALDO: I've never had such a slow-witted apprentice.

COBY: *(Humbly.)* I'm sorry, Waldo.

WALDO: Can't you remember anything? *(Coby hangs his head.)* Repeat the Troll Laws. *(Prompting.)* A troll is two-faced...

COBY: A troll is two-faced. A troll is...*(Hesitates.)*

WALDO: Tricky.

COBY: A troll is tricky. A troll is...

WALDO: Treacherous.

COBY: A troll is treacherous. *(Quickly.)* I remember! A troll is terrible.

WALDO: Say it this way. *(In a deep, ugly voice.)* Terr-ible! *(Coby copies this the best he can.)* That's better. And don't forget it.

COBY: I'll try not to.

In the second scene Coby and Waldo renew their vow to cause as much trouble as possible for "mere mortals."

(A path. This scene may be played in front of the curtain. A spotlight follows Waldo and Coby as they enter from right.)

COBY: I'm tired. *(Sits on rock or the floor.)*

WALDO: A troll should be tireless.

COBY: Is that a Troll Law?

WALDO: Of course.

COBY: Do we have much farther to go?

WALDO: The Bear's castle is just around the corner.

COBY: He really has a castle?

WALDO: He's not an ordinary bear.

COBY: I know that. He's a white bear.

WALDO: Our queen wants him in her power so he'll marry her daughter.

COBY: Ermintrude is so mean.

WALDO: *(Firmly.)* For a troll princess, a mean disposition is a sweet disposition.

COBY: No wonder the White Bear likes Lara.

WALDO: She's a mere mortal.

COBY: We won't hurt her, will we?

WALDO: Who cares?

COBY: I do. She's nice.

WALDO: What kind of troll are you? *(He slaps him on the rump with his stick.)*

COBY: I guess I'm just…well…

WALDO: What kind of a troll am I?

COBY: You're a terrible troll.

WALDO: *(Pleased.)* Right, and all trolls should be just like me.

COBY: I know.

WALDO: Maybe you should be sent to Limbo. *(Slaps him again.)*

COBY: No, no, not that! *(Gets up.)* Don't give up on me, Waldo.

WALDO: Let me hear you say the Troll Motto.

COBY: Be prepared to cause trouble.

WALDO: Now salute and say the Troll Promise.

COBY: *(Puts his left hand to his nose, wiggles his fingers and recites.)* On my honor, I will do my worst... *(Pauses.)*

WALDO: Go on.

COBY: ...to shirk my duty to everyone but my queen...who is ruler of the land East of the Sun and West of the Moon...

WALDO: And?

COBY: To obey the Troll Laws and to hinder mortal people at all times.

WALDO: Our duty is to hinder the girl and the White Bear.

COBY: Even if they're nice?

WALDO: Especially when they're nice. *(He slaps him again.)* How else can a troll be terrible?

COBY: I guess you're right. *(Sits down again.)*

WALDO: On your feet!

COBY: *(Getting up.)* I'll try to do better.

WALDO: Try to do worse. *(Slaps him again.)*

COBY: I'll be much worse.

The Characters: Lara (14) and Justin, The White Bear (ageless)

In this scene Justin, The White Bear, has just refused to go with Coby and Waldo, who have been sent by Helga, Queen of the Trolls, to bring Justin to the castle to marry the Queen's daughter. Justin wants to marry Lara, however.

LARA: Justin, you look angry.

JUSTIN: Not at you.

LARA: Did the little fellows go away?

JUSTIN: Good riddance!

LARA: Is anything wrong?

JUSTIN: I'm not sure. *(She sighs.)* Why the big sigh?

LARA: *(Sitting on stool.)* I just can't help thinking about my family.

JUSTIN: Don't you believe me when I tell you they're all right?

LARA: Oh, yes, I do. But I keep wondering...

JUSTIN: There's no need to.

LARA: My sister Nolly was crying when I left.

JUSTIN: Aren't you happy here?

LARA: I am, I am. *(After a pause.)* But could you take me back so I could see them?

JUSTIN: I have to stay here until midnight.

LARA: Then tell me the way and let me go alone.

JUSTIN: Will you come back?

LARA: I promise I will. I won't stay long.

JUSTIN: A few minutes?

LARA: Maybe half an hour.

JUSTIN: Then it will be dark when you return.

LARA: I'm not afraid of the dark.

JUSTIN: You won't light any candles if I wait up for you?

LARA: I won't, Justin, but why not?

JUSTIN: I can't explain.

LARA: You've been so very good to me, all I ask is a very short visit home.

JUSTIN: *(Walking about.)* I don't know what to say.

LARA: *(Gets up and pets his head.)* Please?

JUSTIN: I'm afraid.

LARA: Of what?

JUSTIN: Something that would cause me great trouble.

LARA: I wouldn't do anything to hurt you.

JUSTIN: Are you sure of that?

LARA: You know I am. I'll say hello to everyone and come right back.

JUSTIN: Then there's a way I can send you there quickly.

LARA: Tell me, please!

JUSTIN: Look in the basket again.

LARA: *(Looking in the basket.)* Oh! *(Takes out a ring.)* A gold ring for my finger!

JUSTIN: It's a gift from my good friend, the sorceress.

LARA: *(Pleased.)* For me?

JUSTIN: To use wisely.

LARA: Oh, I will!

JUSTIN: Put it on.

LARA: *(Putting on the ring.)* It's so pretty. I wish I could meet your friend.

JUSTIN: You already know her.

LARA: How could that be? I've met nobody here.

JUSTIN: If you turn the ring three times, you'll find yourself at home
very soon.

LARA: How wonderful!

JUSTIN: Wait. *(Her hand pauses over the ring.)* I have your promise
to come back?

LARA: You have.

JUSTIN: When you have talked to them all, turn the ring three times
and you'll be here again.

LARA: Oh, thank you, Justin. *(She turns the ring.)* One...two...
three!

THE EMPEROR'S NEW CLOTHES
by Greg Atkins

The Characters: Young Roland (14), Sarah (9) and Mary (13)

This famous tale of a vain Emperor who threatens his town with
poverty in order to provide himself with the finest of clothes, receives
a refreshing new telling in this version. At the center of tricking the
Emperor and saving the town are Young Roland, his clever father, and
Mary, the girl Roland comes to love.

Here Young Roland and Mary seem to be falling in love, which
could prove very helpful to Mary's sister, Sarah.

*(Young Roland runs on and sees Mary hanging out the wash. He
stops and is taken by her beauty, sighs a deep and heartfelt sigh.)*
YOUNG ROLAND: She walks in beauty.

(Mary puts her foot in a bucket of water. Sarah pops up.)
SARAH: She walks in a lot of things.

YOUNG ROLAND: Well, hello there Honest Sarah, how are you?

SARAH: Could be better, could be worse.

YOUNG ROLAND: How could you be better?

SARAH: You could marry my sister so I could have a room all to
myself.

YOUNG ROLAND: You are honest, I'll give you that.

SARAH: Would you like me to talk to her for you?

YOUNG ROLAND: No, I think I can take it from here.

SARAH: Suit yourself, but a word of advice. She hates dishonesty.

YOUNG ROLAND: *(Disheartened.)* Thanks. *(Sarah exits as Young
Roland goes to Mary.)* Good evening, Mary.

(She drops her basket of laundry on his foot.)

MARY: *(Shyly.)* Good evening, Young Roland.

YOUNG ROLAND: You look lovely tonight.

MARY: I thank you.

YOUNG ROLAND: Mary, I have come to ask your help in a very
important matter.

MARY: What is it, Young Roland?

YOUNG ROLAND: If I tell you, you must promise not to tell anyone
about it.

MARY: I promise.

YOUNG ROLAND: *(In a rush.)* I am not a weaver's apprentice. My father and I have deceived the Emperor so we could rob him of his jewels and gold, but I swear to you, if you help us in our endeavor I will make sure that the riches we have taken will be given to the weavers of the city to pay for the Emperor's clothing bills! *(He looks at her hopefully.)*

MARY: Nothing doing.

YOUNG ROLAND: But why? Your sister said you liked honesty.

MARY: As I said before, she is at the age where she is smart enough to tell the truth but too young to know when to say it.

YOUNG ROLAND: Well, if you won't do it for my father and me, then do it for your Aunt.

SARAH: *(Popping up.)* Do it for me! I need my own room.

YOUNG ROLAND: And for Sarah...and the rest of the town.

MARY: All right, I'll help you on one condition.

YOUNG ROLAND: What?

MARY: That after this you stop being a rogue, you settle down in one place, do honest work.

YOUNG ROLAND: *(Unbelievably happy.)* I do. I mean...I will. I think I am falling in love.

MARY: I think I may be too.

SARAH: I think I may be sick.

YOUNG ROLAND and **MARY:** You think too much.

MARY: Let us go quickly! *(They exit.)*

HAPGOOD
by Tom Stoppard

The Characters: Joe (11) and Hapgood (adult)

Joe's mother, Hapgood, is a secret agent for the British government, or is she? This complicated story takes many turns, including mistaken identity and a few dead bodies, before it is over. Young Joe is a boarding student because his mother is away so much. She has surprised him by coming to his rugby game. He's slightly embarrassed because not only is he on the second team but when she attends these games, she cheers too loudly. The game has just finished, when Joe joins his mother on the side lines.

*SPECIAL NOTE: The word "epi" means fit. It isn't really necessary that you use an English accent, just follow the pronunciation of the words as they appear in the scene.

(Joe enters.)
HAPGOOD: Hello, darling.
JOE: Hello, Mum
　　(He is very muddy and glad to see her. His boots are a size too large.)
HAPGOOD: Bad luck – well played anyway. Put this on.
JOE: Thanks.
　　(He takes the tracksuit and puts it on. Hapgood helps him a little.)
[**BLAIR:** Hello, Joe. I'm afraid they were rather good, weren't they?
JOE: Yess'a.
BLAIR: How are you otherwise?
JOE: All rights'a, thank-yous'a. We always get beaten.] I wish you wouldn't watch, Mum.
HAPGOOD: Well, I like watching, I don't mind if you get beaten.
JOE: But nobody watches except you.
HAPGOOD: There's lots of people watching – look over there.
JOE: That the *firsts* – that's what I *mean,* nobody watches Junior Colts B – !
HAPGOOD: I do.
JOE: I *know,* Mum –

HAPGOOD: Well, I won't then.

JOE: I like you *coming* –

HAPGOOD: I didn't shout this time –

JOE: You did a bit, Mum.

HAPGOOD: Hardly at all, whose boots are those?

JOE: Mine.

HAPGOOD: No, they're not.

JOE: Yes they are, I bought them.

HAPGOOD: Where?

JOE: From Sandilands.

HAPGOOD: Who's Sandilands?

JOE: He's had his kidney out so he does computers.

HAPGOOD: Oh. How much?

JOE: A pound.

HAPGOOD: A pound? What was wrong with yours?

JOE: I lost one.

HAPGOOD: You lost a rugby boot?

JOE: Yes. Well, not exactly, I mean I haven't *got* any rugger boots.

HAPGOOD: *(Irked.)* Of course you have, what were you playing in before?

JOE: My hockey shoes – it doesn't matter, nobody minds –

HAPGOOD: You mean you *never* had any rugby boots?

JOE: Only this term, Mother –

HAPGOOD: Why didn't you say? – those look too big anyway, how old is Sandilands?

JOE: *It's all right,* it's silly to buy new boots for Colts B.

HAPGOOD: And now you've lost a hockey shoe? How did that happen?

JOE: It's not lost. It's on the roof.

HAPGOOD: I don't wish to know about this.

JOE: I borrowed the key for Mr. Clark's garage where there's the ladder, I was going to get it down in break with the ladder but I lost it.

HAPGOOD: You lost the ladder?

JOE: No, *the key,* Mum – I put it somewhere and Mr. Clark will have an epi if I don't find it.

HAPGOOD: Is that what you're worried about, Mr. Clark's garage key?

BLAIR: I'll send one of the burglars.

JOE: It's all right, don't *do* anything, Mum –

HAPGOOD: I won't. When was all this?

JOE: Today after breakfast – oh: thank you for the parcel. Your card came, too. When were you in Austria? Did you go to the Spanish horses?

HAPGOOD: No, I was too busy. What was in the parcel?

JOE: The chocolate animals.

HAPGOOD: Oh, yes.

JOE: I gave one to Roger.

HAPGOOD: How is Roger?

JOE: I think he's pregnant.

HAPGOOD: Oh dear.

JOE: Well, he's awfully fat and he only eats chocolate.

HAPGOOD: Oh, well…

JOE: I've got to go –

HAPGOOD: Yes, don't miss tea – have you told Mr. Clark you've lost his garage key?

JOE: No, I mean, he doesn't know I borrowed it.

HAPGOOD: Don't tell him yet – do the grid for me. From getting up, to when you couldn't find it. You remember how we do that?

JOE: It's all right, Mother –

HAPGOOD: I know it's all right. Just do the grid – five minutes for every square, don't leave any out because the key is in one of them, and phone me in first break if you haven't found it.

JOE: Yes, all right, thanks, Mum – thanks for coming –

BLAIR: Goodbye, Joe.

JOE: Goodbyes'a.

HAPGOOD: Bye, darling – I'll let you know when I can come again –

(They exchange a kiss and he runs off.)

LITTLE WOMEN
Adapted by Roger Wheeler
From the Novel by Louisa May Alcott

The Characters: Jo (15) and Beth (13)

Set in Concord, Massachusetts, during the Civil War era, this dramatization of Alcott's popular, uplifting, and very human tale about Jo, Meg, Beth and Amy includes the most memorable scenes from the book. From Jo's writing the Christmas Play and the sisters spending their Christmas money for presents for their mother, through the touching scenes with Beth when the Angel of Death seems near, to the end when the girls are married – Wheeler's adaptation captures the spirit and hope of humankind everywhere.

In the first scene below, Jo discovers Beth curled up in an easy chair, crying softly. It is five o'clock in the evening; dusk.

JO: *(Crosses hastily to right of Beth.)* Why, Beth – you're crying! What on earth – *(Starts to put her arm around Beth.)*

BETH: *(Pushes Jo away.)* You – you better keep away from me, Jo.

JO: *(In amazement.)* Keep away? What do you – ?

BETH: *(Anxiously.)* You've had scarlet fever, haven't you?

JO: *(Mystified.)* Years ago – when Meg did. Why?

BETH: Then I'll tell you. Oh, Jo – the baby's dead! *(Sobs.)*

JO: What baby?

BETH: Mrs. Hummel's! It – it died in my lap before she got home.

JO: *(Tenderly.)* My poor dear – how dreadful for you! I ought to have gone.

BETH: It wasn't dreadful, Jo – only so sad! I saw in a minute that it was sicker, but Lottchen said her mother had gone for a doctor, so I took the baby and let Lotty rest. It seemed asleep, but all of a sudden it gave a little cry, and trembled, and then lay very still. I tried to warm its feet, and Lotty gave it some milk, but it didn't stir, and I knew it was dead. *(Breaks down and sobs.)*

JO: *(Sits on right arm of Beth's chair and puts her arm around her.)* Don't cry, dear! What did you do?

BETH: I just sat and held it softly till Mrs. Hummel came with the doctor. He said it was dead, and looked at Heinrich and Minnie, who have got sore throats. "Scarlet fever, Ma'am! Ought to have called me before," he said crossly. Mrs. Hummel told him she was poor, and had tried to cure the baby herself, but now it was too late, and she could only ask him to help the others, and trust to charity for his pay. He smiled then, and was kinder – but it was very sad. I cried with them till he turned round, all of a sudden, and told me to go home and take belladonna right away, or I'd have the fever.

JO: *(Suddenly frightened – hugs Beth closer.)* No, you won't! Oh, Beth, if you should be sick I never could forgive myself. What *shall* we do?

BETH: Don't be frightened, Jo – I guess I shan't have it badly. *(Indicates book on her lap.)* I looked in Mother's medicine book. It says it begins with headache, sore throat, and queer feelings like mine. I – I took some belladonna, and I – I think I feel better.

JO: *(Runs her hand over Beth's forehead.)* Your head's as hot as fire, Beth.

BETH: *(Closes her eyes and leans back.)* Oooh! How cool your hand is!

JO: *(Worried.)* Oh, if Mother was only at home! You've been holding the baby every day for more than a week, and among the other children who are going to have it. I'm afraid you *are* going to have it, Beth.

BETH: Don't let Amy come near me! She's never had it – and I should hate to give it to her. *(Anxiously.)* Can't you and Meg have it over again?

JO: I guess not! I don't care if I do – serve me right for being a selfish pig to let you go while I could have gone just as well as not. *(Rises.)* Now I'll tell you what we'll do! You get to bed. Then we'll have Dr. Bangs come over and look at you, dear. We'll send Amy off to Aunt March's for a spell, to keep her out of harm's way. I shall stay home and nurse you!

BETH: *(Rises and crosses to Jo at center.)* But, Jo –

JO: Unless you – you'd rather have Meg, Beth.

BETH: *(Puts her arm around Jo and clings to her. Softly.)* No, Jo – I – I'd rather have you, dear – if you don't mind.

JO: *(Holds Beth in a close embrace.)* Oh, Beth!

Four-and-a-half years have elapsed since the scene above. Jo is home visiting with Beth.

(As the curtain rises Beth and Jo are discovered sitting by the fire deep in conversation. Jo sits in the easy chair and Beth sits on the hassock at Jo's feet, her head nestled against Jo's knees. Beth, now four and a half years older since her last appearance, looks frail and wan. She wears a white dress and in the light of the fire there is something almost angelic in her appearance. Jo's hand rests tenderly and lovingly on Beth's shoulder.)

BETH: *(Softly.)* Jo, dear, I'm glad you know it now. I tried to tell you the last time you were home – but I couldn't.

JO: *(Chokes back a sob.)* Oh, Bethy, I –

BETH: I've known it for a good while, dear, and now I'm used to it, it isn't hard to think of or to bear. Try to see it so, and don't be troubled about me, because it's best – indeed it is.

JO: Is this what made you so unhappy last spring, Beth?

BETH: *(Nods.)* Yes, I gave up hoping then, but I didn't like to own it. I tried to think it was a sick fancy – I didn't want to let it trouble anyone. When I saw you all so well and strong, and full of happy plans, it was hard to feel that I could never be like you, and then I was miserable, Jo.

JO: *(Presses Beth's head closer to her.)* Oh, Beth, and you didn't tell me – didn't let me comfort and help you! How could you shut me out, and bear it all alone?

BETH: Perhaps it was wrong, but I tried to do right. I wasn't sure – no one said anything – and I hoped I was mistaken. It would have been selfish to frighten you all when Marmee was so anxious about Meg and the twins, and Amy in Europe, and you so happy with Laurie – at last, I thought so then.

JO: And I thought that you loved him, Beth – and I rushed back to New York and my writing because I couldn't.

BETH: *(Amazed.)* You thought that I –

JO: Then you didn't, dearie? I was afraid it was so – and imagined your poor little heart full of love-lornity all that while.

BETH: *(Innocently looking up at Jo.)* Why, Jo, how could I, when he was so fond of you? I do love Laurie dearly – he was always so good to me – how could I help it? But he never could be anything to me but my brother. I hope he truly will be – sometime.

JO: *(Decidedly.)* Not through me. Amy is left for him – and they'd suit each other excellently.

BETH: Maybe now that Laurie is in Europe too –

JO: Maybe, dear. *(With a change of tone.)* But I've no heart for such things now. I don't care what becomes of anybody but you, Beth. You *must* get well!

BETH: I want to – oh, so much! I try, but every day I lose a little, and feel more sure that I shall never gain it back. It's like the tide, Jo – when it turns, it goes slowly, but it can't be stopped.

JO: *(Desperately.)* It *shall* be stopped! Your tide must not turn so soon – eighteen is too young. Beth, I can't let you go! I'll work and pray and fight against it! I'll keep you in spite of everything! There must be ways – it can't be too late. God won't be so cruel to take you from me!

BETH: *(With a sob.)* I try to be willing to go, but –

JO: *(Breaks down.)* Oh, Bethy! *(Clings closer to Beth and sobs for a moment.)*

BETH: You'll tell Marmee and Father – when they get home?

JO: I think they'll see it without words, Beth.

BETH: Perhaps not! I've heard that the people who love best are often blindest to such things. If they don't see it – you tell them for me. I don't want any secrets, and it's kinder to prepare them. Meg has John and the babies to comfort her, but you must stand by Father and Mother – won't you, Jo? *(Looks up wistfully at Jo.)*

JO: If I can! But, Beth – I don't give up yet. I'm going to believe that it *is* a sick fancy – and not let you think it's true.

BETH: *(After a moment's pause.)* I don't know how to express myself, and shouldn't try to anyone but you – because I can't speak out, except to my Jo. I only mean to say that I have a feeling that it never was intended I should live long. I'm not like the rest of you. I never made any plans about what I'd do when I grew up. I never thought of being married as you all did. I couldn't seem to imagine myself anything but stupid little Beth, trotting about at home, of no use anywhere but here. I never wanted to go away, and the hard part now is the leaving you all. I'm not afraid – but it seems as if I should be homesick for you even in heaven. *(There is a long pause. Then suddenly.)* Jo – do you remember the little canary I used to have? The one that died – and we buried out in the garden?

JO: *(Very choky.)* Yes, Beth.

BETH: And do you remember the little epitaph you wrote for him. *(Recites.)*

"Here lies Pip March,
    Who died the seventh of June;
Loved and lamented sore,
    And not forgotten soon."

JO: Don't – Beth!

BETH: All I wanted to say, Jo – was that we're like a family of birds – different kinds. You're like a gull, Jo, strong and wild, fond of the storm and the wind, flying far out to sea, and happy all alone. Meg's the turtle-dove – and Amy's like the lark, trying to get up among the clouds, but always dropping down into its nest again. Dear little girl! She's so ambitious, but her heart is good and tender – and no matter how high she flies, she never will forget home. *(Sighs.)* I hope I shall see her again – but she seems so far away.

JO: *(With an attempt at cheerfulness.)* She is coming in the spring – and I mean that you shall be ready to see and enjoy her. I'm going to have you well and rosy by that time.

BETH: *(Tries to smile.)* Jo, dear, don't hope any more! It won't do you any good – I'm sure of that. We won't be miserable, but enjoy being together while we wait. We'll have happy times – for I don't suffer much, and I think the tide will go out easily, if you help me. *(Jo, unable to speak, bends down and kisses Beth.)* Do you want me to play something, Jo? *(Jo nods. Beth rises and crosses to piano. Sits down and starts to play a hymn. Stops after a few notes – turns to Jo.)* Jo?

JO: Yes, Beth?

BETH: Do you mind if – if Meg has my piano? I – I promised it to her that time when I had scarlet fever, you know. *(She starts to play the hymn again as the curtain falls slowly.)*

MAKE A FRIEND, FIND A FRIEND
by Paul Maar
translated by Anita and Alex Page

The Characters: Stephen (11-12) and Fantasy Figure (ageless)

Stephen has lived with only his father for many years. Recently his father married Varnia, whom he met while traveling. The three have moved to a new community and Stephen has become introverted, preferring to stay in his room and play rather than socialize. Still, he longs for a friend. He is particularly interested in Katy, but is shy and awkward about developing the friendship. To make matters more difficult Mike, the neighborhood bully, keeps getting in Stephen's way in his attempts to make friends with Katy. Privately, Stephen invents a fantasy friend who helps strengthen his resolve and encourages Stephen to take charge of his life. The Fantasy Figure is capable of "playing" other people in Stephen's life and, in the process, Stephen sorts out the resolutions to this problems.

In this first scene, the Fantasy Figure helps boost Stephen's confidence.

(Stephen looks in his backpack for the science textbook and discovers Katy's scarf, which he had kept in order to return it to her next morning in school. He pulls out the scarf, examines it, and holds it like a precious object. Behind him, the slats of the blind turn, and Fantasy Figure becomes visible and stares, like him, at the scarf.)

STEPHEN: You!

FANTASY FIGURE: What?

STEPHEN: What would you say if you were Katy and I was returning your scarf?

FANTASY FIGURE: You...you've saved my scarf.

(During the following brief dialogue, Stephen does not glance at Fantasy Figure. He holds the scarf in his hand, lost in a dream, while Fantasy Figure responds. It should become clear that Fantasy Figure expresses what he imagines. Perhaps he might even mouth inaudibly the first few replies. Stephen is extremely serious about each statement; both speak intensely and familiarly, even though – seen objectively – they are quite sentimental.

Moreover, Fantasy Figure wears the same sweater as Katy.)

STEPHEN: I saved it for you so Mike wouldn't grab it again.

FANTASY FIGURE: You did it for me?

STEPHEN: I quickly ran away with it.

FANTASY FIGURE: I'll never forget you for it, never.

STEPHEN: *(A little embarrassed in his pride.)* Wasn't all that hard.

FANTASY FIGURE: I'll never forget you for it, if I live to be a hundred.

STEPHEN: Honest?

FANTASY FIGURE: I swear.

STEPHEN: You're going to be an old woman when you're a hundred.

(Only now does he look at Fantasy Figure and puts the scarf on her head, like the babushka of an old woman. Slowly the tone changes; it becomes gay, playful.)

FANTASY FIGURE: I am sure to be using a cane, like this. *(She demonstrates.)*

STEPHEN: *(Once again serious.)* And even so, you haven't forgotten.

FANTASY FIGURE: *(As an old woman.)* Never! But by then you too will be walking with a cane. Because you'll be a hundred years old.

STEPHEN: I guess so. *(He becomes a hundred-year-old man.)* Katy!

FANTASY FIGURE: Stevie!

STEPHEN: Do you remember how, way back when, I saved your scarf?

FANTASY FIGURE: The scarf, yes, I do. *(They nod, wistful and trembling.)*

STEPHEN: *(In the broken voice of an old man.)* Listen, Katy, I've got to do some more homework.

FANTASY FIGURE: Math?

STEPHEN: Done my math. *(Whispers in her ear.)* I'll let you copy it. – No, still got to do my science.

FANTASY FIGURE: The tiger.

STEPHEN: Mr. Miller said we should keep it short and to the point. First, the title: The Tiger.

FANTASY FIGURE: That's to the point.

STEPHEN: Yes, Let's write that down.

(Stephen begins to write while Fantasy Figure looks with him into the notebook. They are no longer hundred-year-olds but two

school kids who are doing their homework together.)

FANTASY FIGURE: First we write how the tiger looks, then where he lives.

STEPHEN: The tiger has streaks.

FANTASY FIGURE: He resides in the jungle.

STEPHEN: "Resides" is bad. It sounds as though he had a four-room apartment.

FANTASY FIGURE: The tiger streaks through the jungle. "The tiger has streaks and streaks through the jungle."

STEPHEN: No, even better: "The streaky tiger streaks through the jungle."

FANTASY FIGURE: That is to the point.

STEPHEN: Let's write it down. – How do we go on from there? How about this? He is very dangerous and very long.

FANTASY FIGURE: Quite good. But Miller will certainly want to know *how* long he is.

STEPHEN: *(Doubtful.)* Five yards?

FANTASY FIGURE: I think longer.

STEPHEN: Right.

(Both look at an eight-yard imaginary tiger on the stage, counting off each yard by a nod.)

STEPHEN: *(Decided.)* Eight. He is very dangerous and eight yards long…What if that isn't so?

FANTASY FIGURE: I got it. Let's right: The tiger is dangerously long.

STEPHEN: To the point! Now, Katy, we come to his food.

FANTASY FIGURE: I think he eats monkeys.

STEPHEN: But when he gets old and can't catch them any more, he creeps into a village and attacks people. Or steals chickens. How do we put that?

FANTASY FIGURE: If he doesn't get monkeys, he gobbles people or chickens.

STEPHEN: "Gobbles" doesn't sound right. One can't gobble people. Sounds gross.

FANTASY FIGURE: If he doesn't get monkeys, he *consumes* people or chickens.

STEPHEN: Very good. Now we have to write about a tiger hunt.

FANTASY FIGURE: That's easy. They hunt him.

STEPHEN: No. That sounds as though the chickens are hunting him. *(He laughs.)* Just imagine, two chickens in sun-helmets and guns on a tiger hunt.

(They play two chickens who creep cackling through the jungle and screech in excitement as they discover the tiger and kill him.)

FANTASY FIGURE: True, you can't say that. What if we leave out the chickens. He consumes people who hunt him down.

STEPHEN: If they're consumed, they can't hunt him.

FANTASY FIGURE: Then let's leave out the people too and write only about the tiger.

STEPHEN: How?

FANTASY FIGURE: After his meal, the tiger has to reckon with being hunted.

STEPHEN: Sounds good. Like from the science textbook. That's exactly how I'm going to write it. *(He says the words as he writes.)* The streaky tiger streaks through the jungle. He is dangerously long. After eating, he must reckon with being hunted.

In this second scene, the Fantasy Figure role-plays Mike to help Stephen sort out his fears and overcome them.

(The hall door slams. Stephen returns from school, throws his backpack on the floor, and gives it a kick. He is furious.)

STEPHEN: So mean! *(Furious, he yells for Fantasy Figure.)* Hey!

FANTASY FIGURE: *(Glancing through the blind.)* Hi, Stephen.

STEPHEN: You're supposed to be Mike.

FANTASY FIGURE: Mike?

STEPHEN: Don't ask so many questions. Yes!

(Fantasy Figure disappears behind the blind. Stephen walks about the room agitated, thinks aloud about Mike.)

STEPHEN: Today he had that phony baseball jacket on again…And those red pants…I should've hid the note better. As it was…

(He withdraws the note from his pocket and looks at it. Fantasy Figure enters as Mike and is dressed like him. In the posture characteristic of Mike he ambles to Stephen.)

FANTASY FIGURE/MIKE: What's that piece of paper?

(Stephen tries to hide it, but Mike has managed to snatch it from his hand. He reads aloud.) "To Katy from Stephen."

STEPHEN: Gimme that!

FANTASY FIGURE: *(Reads aloud with his comments.)* "Dear Katy"

...Get it, *Dear!* "That business with the scarf was quite different..."

STEPHEN: The letter isn't any business of yours!

FANTASY FIGURE: "I wanted to save it for you." Save it! Such slop. Scarf saved from mortal danger by rescue helicopter. Ta-ta-ta-taaah! "So Mike wouldn't grab it again." *(Addressing Stephen.)* Listen, if I'd *wanted* the scarf, I'd have gotten it. You can bet on that.

(He licks the note and plasters it contemptuously on Stephen's cheek, then he leaves the [class] room. We feel that the scene just played agrees with the one that actually occurred. But Stephen now gives it a new turn.)

STEPHEN: *(Loud and firm.)* Stop!

FANTASY FIGURE: *(Turns, bewildered.)* You mean me?

STEPHEN: Who else, jerk head! *(He likes the sentence so much that he repeats it.)* Who else, jerk head!

FANTASY FIGURE: What's the matter? Popped one of your fuses? D'you have any idea who you're talking to?

STEPHEN: Only too well, you skunk. But I'm afraid you don't know who *you're* talking to. Who am I?

FANTASY FIGURE: *(Irritated.)* You nuts? Stephen, of course.

STEPHEN: *(Amused.)* Stephen? Well, that's what they call me in the land of the setting sun. But my friends call me Stee-Fa-Nang.

FANTASY FIGURE: *(Alarmed.)* Stee-Fa-Nang, the Fighter?

STEPHEN: Exactly.

FANTASY FIGURE: Can't be true!

STEPHEN: *(Rips open his coat, his back to the audience.)* And what is that?

FANTASY FIGURE: The four claws!

STEPHEN: *(Pointing to his chest.)* The red – the silver – the gold. And here!

FANTASY FIGURE: *(Anxiously.)* The invisible!

STEPHEN: The invisible claw! Only three in the entire world are allowed to wear it: Kung-Lang-Fu, Lo-Chi-Min, and...

FANTASY FIGURE: *(In a dying voice.)* Stee-Fa-Nang!

STEPHEN: *(Closes his coat, nods imperiously.)* Exactly.

FANTASY FIGURE: *(Trying to rise again.)* You stole it. You are not Stee-Fa-Nang...

(Stephen, with loud battle cries, carries out three karate attacks against Fantasy Figure/Mike, who hides behind the couch,

terrified.)

FANTASY FIGURE: Mercy, Stee-Fa-Nang, mercy!

STEPHEN: You know that you've lost. Still, I don't thirst for revenge. I'll save you.

FANTASY FIGURE: Thank you, Stee-Fa-Nang.

STEPHEN: But a little lesson I will teach you. You will write a hundred times: "I am not permitted to read Stephen's letters out loud." Begin! Now!

FANTASY FIGURE: Yes, Stephen. Where am I supposed to write it?

STEPHEN: Here, on your knees.

FANTASY FIGURE: On my knees, of course, Stephen.
(Stephen hands him a piece of paper from his backpack, and Fantasy Figure begins to write eagerly.)
I am not permitted to read Stephen's letter out loud. I am not...

STEPHEN: Speed it up!

FANTASY FIGURE: Speed, yes, Stephen, speed. *(He writes with furious speed.)*

The Characters: Stephen (11-12) and Katy (11-12)

In this scene, Stephen gets help from a "real friend" for the first time, which changes his life forever.

(Stephen and Katy, coming from outside, enter room.)

STEPHEN: Lucky I had the key, otherwise we would never have gotten in.

KATY: *(Looking around.)* Are these your books?

STEPHEN: Yep.

KATY: *(Reading.)* "The Alien Planet" – I have a book like that. Mine is called "On Alien Stars." In mine, they land on a star, where the people don't have any eyes.

STEPHEN: So how can they see?

KATY: By electricity, or something like that.

STEPHEN: On my planet the inhabitants are giant spiders who can speak.

KATY: Spiders? That's spinning something! You know, we can play and pretend we're on an unknown star.

STEPHEN: Yeah! We fly there.

KATY: *(Jumps on a chair and down.)* Why? We're already there.

STEPHEN: *(Does as she does. But it does not satisfy him. His play fantasies lie in another direction.)* No, we've got to have a spaceship. This here is our spaceship, o.k.? I am the captain and you...

KATY: How come you're the captain?

STEPHEN: Who else?

KATY: Me.

STEPHEN: Impossible. The captain is always a man.

KATY: In that case I am the woman captain.

STEPHEN: *(Almost helpless.)* And me?

KATY: O.k. You're the captain.

STEPHEN: Take your seat. Fire the motors! Countdown: ten, nine, eight, seven, six, five, four, three, two, one – go!
(They produce starting sounds. Once they're beyond them Katy assumes they have landed. She gets out and looks amazed around the alien star. In the meantime, Stephen continues the game he is accustomed to play with Fantasy Figure.)

STEPHEN: Computer log: December 13, 2037. Hey, Katy, first we've got to land.

KATY: Oh yes, land. *(She resumes her seat.)*

STEPHEN: After a flight of three years, we are approaching an unknown planet in the galaxy Beta/2/Y. Coordinates, please! Please, the coordinates!
(Katy, who has no idea what is meant by coordinates, brings two caps [or two pillows, or something similar.])

STEPHEN: *(Whispering to her.)* No, you have to give me numbers.

KATY: I get it. Seven, nine, twenty-eight, fourteen, eleven, three, hundred ninety-two, four, three, eighteen...

STEPHEN: That's enough.

KATY: ...twenty, eight...

STEPHEN: Hold it. Prepare for landing.

KATY: Ready for landing.

STEPHEN: We're landing.
(They act out a hard impact landing.)

STEPHEN: We managed to get the old crate down all right, didn't we? – Got to test the planet's atmosphere.

KATY: *(Raises a finger, licks it.)* Atmosphere clean.

STEPHEN: Clean? Then we don't need spacesuits.

(Katy has already descended. Now she is in charge of the game and she plays it according to her kind of inventiveness. The following game should have a quality other than that of Stephen's with his Fantasy Figure. In her version, Katy changes the environment into an imaginary planet. In contrast to Stephen's fantasy games, which always made use of many objects (backpack as oxygen tank, goldfish bowl as helmet, playing cards, etc.) she succeeds in creating an alien world entirely by the power of her imagination. Stephen is hesitant at first, but gradually he becomes more excited and absorbed.)

KATY: *(Full of wonder.)* Take a look at that, Steve! Red grass!
(He looks down while she looks up. Her grass is at least ten feet tall. She works her way through the grass as he follows her hesitantly and clumsily.)

KATY: And the little trees.
(Stephen looks up at the trees. But Katy has squatted down in order to pluck the trees. She hands him a bouquet which he stares at amazed. Katy continues her trek through the grass.)

KATY: Steve! Hey, I'm growing, I'm getting taller. Can you still see me, Steve?

STEPHEN: *(Squatting very low and looking straight up.)* Hello, Katy!

KATY: Hi, Steve! *(She shouts as though way up high.)* Come up here, then you'll grow too. I can already look over the grass.

STEPHEN: *(Follows her and grows too.)* Me, too.

KATY: Back there are the mountains. Come on up, here we can look over the mountains. *(They climb on an armchair or chair [or something similar] and look at the mountains, overcome.)*

STEPHEN: Beautiful. Katy, hey, Katy, something is pulling me down.

KATY: Hold on. *(She holds him by his hand as he is lying on the table looking down.)*

STEPHEN: A pit! You saved me!

KATY: *(Lies next to him, looking down.)* How deep is it, do you think?
(In pantomime they drop a stone, then listen to the sound of the stone falling. It takes a long time until it hits bottom.)

KATY: Wow, is that ever deep!

STEPHEN: And wide too. *(He looks into the distance.)*
(They look together into the infinite abyss.)

KATY: You think one could get across?

STEPHEN: Never.

KATY: We could fly…

STEPHEN: With the space ship?

KATY: No. I mean, really.

(Stephen raises Katy to his shoulders, stands on the table, his arms spread. He has a moment of doubt.)

STEPHEN: Do you think it'll work?

KATY: If you trust yourself!

STEPHEN: *(Determined.)* Let's go!

(Both have spread their arms wide and simulate the slow turning of bird's wings. Their concentration is intense, their breathing keeps time. The sound of their breathing turns gently into the sound of wind [produced from a tape], so gently that it is impossible to say whether it originates from the two or from the tape, or whether we only imagine it, because the intimation of flying is so effective. From the first "beating of the wings" the lights begin to dim until the stage is entirely dark. Music.)

THE MAN-CHILD
by Arnold Rabin

The Characters: Allen (12) and Herb (12)

The Man-Child is the coming of age story of a young Jewish boy, Allen, who is about to have his Bar Mitzvah. Through the telling of Allen's wise old grandmother, Mrs. Wishnefsky, we live out the challenges that confront Allen during the days preceding his rite of passage, from almost losing his dress suit to the telling of a lie that turns the boy against his mother. In the end, these tests prove that Allen is indeed ready to become a man.

Here Allen has received a prized gift which he is about to show his good friend, Herb.

ALLEN: Hi, Herb –

HERB: Hi – you nervous?

ALLEN: Not too... *(A slight pause.)* Guess what.

HERB: I don't know. *(Pause.)* What do you have your hand behind your back for?

ALLEN: That's part of it.

HERB: Is it in your hand what you want to show me?

ALLEN: You're getting hot! Not "in" my hand.

HERB: Is it one of those new kind of watches that you can put on your wrist?

ALLEN: No...that's for millionaires. But it's almost as good.

HERB: What is it then?

ALLEN: *(Taking his hand from behind his back.)* It's a ring. It belonged to my father. It's his Bar Mitzvah ring. And it's gold!

HERB: Real gold?

ALLEN: Real gold!

HERB: *(A shot of envy races through him.)* How do you know it's real gold?

ALLEN: My mother told me when she gave it to me!

HERB: Does it say so on the ring?

ALLEN: What do you mean?

HERB: It says so if it's real gold.

ALLEN: Yeah, I didn't look.

HERB: Sure, my brother got a ring from my uncle when he graduated and inside it had a 14K. It stands for fourteen karat.

ALLEN: That's what my mother said this was.

HERB: It should say so inside. If it doesn't say so, it's not real gold.

ALLEN: Well, I'm not worried. I'm sure it is.

HERB: I'll show you where it said so on my brother's ring. It was right on the side – underneath.

ALLEN: *(Covering the ring hand again.)* I don't want to take it off.

HERB: You're going to have to take it off sometime. When you wash your hands you'll have to take it off.

ALLEN: Maybe – but I don't want to take it off just like that.

HERB: You could, just for a second. It wouldn't hurt. See if it says 14K like my brother's. That's the real test. You can put it right back on.

ALLEN: I don't have to test it. I know it's real gold!

HERB: Well, I don't. You're asking me to take your word!

ALLEN: It's not my word! It's my father's ring! And my mother wouldn't tell me it was fourteen karat if it wasn't.

HERB: How do I know she told you it was? You might have just made it up. You might have made up the whole story.

ALLEN: *(Hurt at the insinuation.)* I didn't make it up! Why would I do that!

HERB: Lots of reasons. So I should think you had something that was real gold when you didn't.

ALLEN: But it is real gold! How many times do I have to tell you?

HERB: Then let me see it where it should say so. That's all I'm asking. If it has the 14K – *(Impulsively Allen removes the ring from his finger. He looks inside. Herb immediately tries to look too.)* Do you see it?

ALLEN: Take it easy.

HERB: It's hard sometimes. *(Allen turns the ring in several directions. Then Herb grabs it from him.)* Let me look, I got better eyes. *(He studies the ring carefully.)* I don't see nothing. *(Allen takes the ring back. He looks again himself.)*

ALLEN: It's probably rubbed off. It's old. Twenty-six years old. And I guess those things rub off after a while. I know a cousin of mine had a ring with his initials on the side and after a couple of years they were all rubbed away.

HERB: They scratch the 14K pretty deep. It's important for them, so even if you couldn't read it clear, there should be some sign of it.

And I don't see any sign.

ALLEN: It is real gold! I know it is. My mother wouldn't have told me otherwise!

HERB: You don't think she'd give you a ring and tell you it was a fake, do you!

ALLEN: It's not a fake!

HERB: All I know is – it doesn't say 14K!

ALLEN: They could have left it off, couldn't they! There's no law that says they have to put it on, is there?

HERB: *(Deliberately.)* I don't know if there's a law, but if it's real gold, jewelers put it on!

ALLEN: Well, my ring's from the old country. Maybe there –

HERB: It doesn't matter where it comes from.

ALLEN: *(Not really knowing how –)* I can prove it's gold.

HERB: How?

ALLEN: *(Hedging.)* There are ways to prove it's gold without it saying 14K.

HERB: If there is, I don't know it.

ALLEN: Then that shows how much you know! There's got to be a way! Else how could a jeweler know it's fourteen karat before he puts the 14K on it! There must be a test! Somebody's got to have a way to find out in the beginning!

HERB: Maybe. I guess they do have some kind of test. *(Pause.)* Maybe they try to dent it. You know like they do with coins! You've seen them put the coins between their teeth!

ALLEN: Do you think that would be a test?

HERB: It works with coins. Try it!

ALLEN: If it doesn't dent, will you believe it's fourteen karat even if it doesn't have the 14K?

HERB: I guess so. It would be proof!

(Allen stares at the ring. He takes it between his fingers. Slowly he brings it to his mouth. There is one last hesitation.)

ALLEN: I know it's real gold!

HERB: Prove it – go ahead – Bite it! See if it dents! *(Allen places the ring between his teeth and closes his teeth down on the ring. Then he cups his hand over his mouth and lets the ring drop into it. Slowly he opens his fist.)* It's dented! I told you it wasn't real gold! I told you it had to say 14K! I told you it was a fake! *(Allen stares at the dented ring. The light fades.)*

THE MEMBER OF THE WEDDING
by Carson McCullers

The Characters: Frankie (12) and John Henry (8)

Adapted from her novel of the same name, Carson McCullers tells the coming of age story of Frankie, a somewhat awkward and out-of-sorts little girl in search of her place in the world. Her mother is dead, her father hasn't much time for her, and she's too hot-tempered to make friends with other girls. Much of her time is spent with Berenice, the family's warm-hearted cook, and John Henry, her little cousin, but she is looking forward to much more in life.

In the scene below Berenice, who is leaving for the night, has just told Frankie to go play with John Henry until Mr. Addams, Frankie's father, comes home. Frankie has a lot on her mind.

FRANKIE: Seems like everybody goes off and leaves me. *(She walks towards the Wests' yard, calling, with cupped hands.)* John Henry. John Henry.

JOHN HENRY'S VOICE: What do you want, Frankie?

FRANKIE: Come over and spend the night with me.

JOHN HENRY'S VOICE: I can't.

FRANKIE: Why?

JOHN HENRY: Just because.

FRANKIE: Because why? *(John Henry does not answer.)* I thought maybe me and you could put up my Indian tepee and sleep out here in the yard. And have a good time. *(There is still no answer.)* Sure enough. Why don't you stay and spend the night?

JOHN HENRY: *(Quite loudly.)* Because, Frankie, I don't want to.

FRANKIE: *(Angrily.)* Fool Jackass! Suit yourself! I only asked you because you looked so ugly and so lonesome.

JOHN HENRY: *(Skipping toward the arbor.)* Why, I'm not a bit lonesome.

FRANKIE: *(Looking at the house.)* I wonder when that Papa of mine is coming home. He always comes home by dark. I don't want to go into that empty, ugly house all by myself.

JOHN HENRY: Me neither.

FRANKIE: *(Standing with outstretched arms, and looking around* *her.)* I think something is wrong. It is too quiet. I have a peculiar warning in my bones. I bet you a hundred dollars it's going to storm.

JOHN HENRY: I don't want to spend the night with you.

FRANKIE: A terrible, terrible dog-day storm. Or maybe even a cyclone.

JOHN HENRY: Huh.

FRANKIE: I bet Jarvis and Janice are now at Winter Hill. I see them just plain as I see you. Plainer. Something is wrong. It is too quiet. *(A clear horn begins to play a blues tune in the distance.)*

JOHN HENRY: Frankie?

FRANKIE: Hush! It sounds like Honey.

(The horn music becomes jazzy and spangling, then the first blues tune is repeated. Suddenly, while still unfinished, the music stops. Frankie waits tensely.)

FRANKIE: He has stopped to bang the spit out of his horn. In a second he will finish. *(After a wait.)* Please, Honey, go on finish!

JOHN HENRY: *(Softly.)* He done quit now.

FRANKIE: *(Moving restlessly.)* I told Berenice that I was leavin' town for good and she did not believe me. Sometimes I honestly think she is the biggest fool that ever drew breath. You try to impress something on a big fool like that, and it's just like talking to a block of cement. I kept on telling and telling her. I told her I had to leave this town for good because it is inevitable. Inevitable.

THE NICKEL
by Charles Webb

The Characters: Herbie and Ralph (two fifth-grade boys)

Poor Herbie. This is one of the worst days of his life, a life that isn't all that exciting or rewarding either. He returns to school to find that everyone in class thinks he was killed in a hold-up. When they took a collection for flowers for his grave, it turned out to be only a nickel. There seem to be no friends, and his teacher, Ms. Peterson, is a grouch who can't get his name right (she calls him Alfonso).

In this scene, Herbie has been sent to the principal's office. As he waits, his "best friend," Ralph, comes by to see him.

(Lights up on principal's office lobby stage left. Open door to hall is upstage left. Shut door to principal's office is stage left. Upstage on wall is a large circular clock. Sound of Ralph walking quickly down the hall toward stage left. He stops just before he reaches the door.)

RALPH: *(From hall to Herbie.)* Alfonso. What are you doing outside the principal's office? Walker will let out in a few minutes.

HERBIE: *(From hall to Ralph, depressed.)* Hi, Ralph. I have to see Mr. Hano.

RALPH: *(Uncaring.)* Oh yeah. Tough luck. Say, you can't wait out here. You got to sign in.

HERBIE: I did. I just had to go to the bathroom and throw up.

RALPH: You must have taken hot lunch today.

HERBIE: Fortunately the main course crawled off my plate before I had a chance to eat it.

(Herbie and Ralph enter the lobby of the principal's office.)

HERBIE: By the way, thanks for the nickel.

RALPH: What nickel?

(A couple of kids walk down the hall to the exit.)

HERBIE: For the flowers.

RALPH: That wasn't me.

HERBIE: But you're my best friend.

RALPH: I don't doubt that. But I didn't pay any money in the collection can.

(The kids exit the building. Sound of big city noises can be heard whenever the school doors are open.)

HERBIE: *(Puzzled.)* But...

RALPH: I'm saving my bread for something real important.

HERBIE: A Corvette?

RALPH: No. College.

(A kid walks rapidly down the hall to the exit.)

HERBIE: I suppose tuition will be high when...

RALPH: *(Impatient.)* My parents will pay that. They owe it to me.

(The kid opens and exits the school doors.)

HERBIE: Then what?

RALPH: Beer money. I want to make sure I'll be able to afford to hang out with the right crowd.

HERBIE: Drunks?

RALPH: If I expect to rake in mega bucks as a shrink, I need to make contacts.

HERBIE: I didn't know you were going to be a psychiatrist.

RALPH: *(Matter of fact.)* Why do you think I waste so much time with you?

HERBIE: *(Hurt.)* I thought you...felt sorry for me. Or maybe, even liked me. A little.

RALPH: *(Laughing.)* That's a good one.

HERBIE: Then why?

RALPH: Most nut cases were losers as kids. I figure by the time I open my practice, you'll be even worse off than you are now.

(A few kids hurry down the hall to the exit.)

RALPH: And assuming you don't blow out what's left of your brains, or are committed to a state mental hospital, you'll be in the market for an analysis.

(The kids open the school door and leave. Herbie looks at his feet, then slowly up to Ralph.)

HERBIE: If you didn't give me the nickel, then who?

RALPH: What difference does it make? *(Looks at clock on the wall.)* I'm out of here.

(Ralph starts to walk away. Herbie grabs Ralph's arm. Ralph stops.)

HERBIE: Please, you've got to help me. You know everybody in our class.

RALPH: Hey, watch it. *(He shakes his arm free from Herbie's grip.)* You could hurt my arm grabbing it like that. I'll be needing it to write prescriptions for anti-depressants.

HERBIE: *(Smiles.)* Sorry.

RALPH: I suppose I can tell you what I know. I don't want you to have a mental breakdown before I'm able to cash in on it.

HERBIE: *(Smiles.)* Thanks.

RALPH: None of the guys said anything about putting any money in the can. And I know none of the girls would.

HERBIE: *(Defensive.)* Why not?

RALPH: They wouldn't want anyone to think they were in love with you or something.

(A couple of kids run down the hall to the exit.)

HERBIE: But if everyone thought I was dead, what difference would it make?

RALPH: They have their pride.

(The kids open the school doors and exit.)

HERBIE: You don't suppose it was...Ms. Peterson?

RALPH: You can definitely rule her out.

HERBIE: Yeah. She doesn't seem to care a whole lot for me.

RALPH: Doesn't care for you? She despises your very being.

HERBIE: *(Frustrated.)* Then who?

RALPH: *(Guessing.)* The janitor?

HERBIE: I don't think so. Every time I'm in the hall, he sticks out his broom and tries to trip me.

RALPH: How come?

HERBIE: I think he blames me for breaking my chair. But it was already broken when I...

RALPH: *(Amazed.)* I never thought I'd say this. I mean, it doesn't seem possible.

HERBIE: *(Excited.)* What?

RALPH: *(In disbelief.)* Someone must actually like you.

HERBIE: You mean a secret admirer?

RALPH: I wouldn't go as far as that. After all, it was just a nickel.

HERBIE: *(Let down.)* Oh.

RALPH: But I would definitely say *like*.

HERBIE: *(Pleased.)* Yeah.

RALPH: Perhaps you aren't the only potential client in our class.

(Sound of civil defense siren going off nearby.)

RALPH: Walker's letting out! I'd stay and walk home with you, but no sense in both of us getting mutilated. *(He dashes down the hall to the exit.)* Farewell Alfonso.

(Herbie stands in the open doorway and watches Ralph go. He waves slightly at him. When Ralph opens the school doors, there is the sound of several children running down the street screaming. Herbie cringes at what he sees.)

PAINTED RAIN
by Janet Allard

The Characters: Teddy (11) and Dustin (16)

Janet Allard was fifteen when she wrote this one-act play and
submitted it to the Foundation of the Dramatists Guild's annual Young
Playwrights Festival. The play was one of six plays selected for
production at the Playwrights Horizons in 1989. *Painted Rain* is the
story of two foster children, Teddy, a sensitive and creative boy, and
his roommate, Dustin, an angry yet talented young painter confined to
a wheelchair. Over the course of several scenes the relationship
between the boys and their social worker, Barbara, leads to a deeper
appreciation of life and the need to help one another.

In scene four, Teddy, who is about to be taken from the foster home,
has been packing his belongings. He is going to miss Dustin, whom he
has come to regard as his older brother.

*(The stage is dimly lit. Dustin is lying in bed sleeping, and Teddy
is packing a suitcase that is lying open on his bed. He is talking
to no one in particular as he is packing. The sound of rain hitting
against the windowpane is noticeable, but soft. It will grow more
noticeable as the scene progresses.)*

TEDDY: Ya know, sometimes I think it really wouldn't be so bad to
be blind. You wouldn't have to worry about what everything
looked like. You could make things look like you wanted them to.
You could wear clothes that didn't match, and nobody would tell
you you had no taste. They would think you dressed like that just
'cause you couldn't see. If we couldn't see, we'd start seeing the
things inside people more.
*(Teddy stops packing and wanders over to Dustin's easel. Picking
up a paintbrush, he goes back to his bed, reaches under it, pulls
out his bag of stuff, and adds the paintbrush to his collection.
Teddy picks up the suitcase and walks to the door. Putting the
suitcase down, he turns to look at Dustin.)*

TEDDY: Dustin? *(Silence.)* You awake, Dustin? *(Silence.)* Dustin?

DUSTIN: *(Annoyed.)* What?

TEDDY: I want to talk to you.

DUSTIN: It's two o'clock in the morning. Go to sleep!

TEDDY: What's wrong?

DUSTIN: Just go to sleep.

TEDDY: Dustin? I'm leaving tomorrow. I want to talk to you.

DUSTIN: I'll talk to you in the morning. Now, go lie down.

TEDDY: Dustin –

DUSTIN: Teddy – leave me alone.

TEDDY: Dustin? *(When Dustin doesn't answer, Teddy reaches up and gently puts his hand on Dustin's face. Dustin bolts to a sitting position.)*

DUSTIN: Quit it! You're not blind.

TEDDY: I'm cold. Just hold me a minute. *(The two boys look at each other for a minute, then Dustin turns over and lies down again, with his back to Teddy.)* Dustin…this is the last time…this is the last time…Can't you just…Forget it! This is the last time you'll see me. I'm the only thing you have, and I'm leaving.

DUSTIN: Good! Now, go to sleep.

(Teddy turns away and goes back to his bed. He curls up and softly begins crying. Dustin is silent for a while. He then pulls himself into his wheelchair, talking softly to Teddy.)

DUSTIN: I used to think that the morning light was yellow. That's the color streetlights are and the color the moon is and everything. Then one night I woke up and looked around. It was two o'clock, and it was blue. You know what I wanted to do, Teddy? I wanted to wake you up and show you that everything was blue, not yellow like I thought. But I didn't. It's different tonight. Everything should be blue in here, but it's not. Maybe I should paint the sky yellow, like you said, and red. Yeah, a red splash could mix in just fine. *(By this time the rain can be heard against the windowpane. Dustin has gotten into his wheelchair and now wheels over to Teddy's bed.)* Teddy? *(Pause.)* I need you. I'm scared.

TEDDY: *(Looks up and then goes to Dustin and sits in his lap.)* It's raining, Dustin. I can hear it.

DUSTIN: Yes, it's raining.

TEDDY: But you can't see it…no one can.

DUSTIN: It's too dark to see at night. You can hear it, and if you went outside, you could feel it.

TEDDY: I can feel it.

DUSTIN: Then let's paint it.

(Teddy gets a canvas, palette, and brush and brings it to Dustin.

Dustin puts Teddy's hand on his own, holding the brush. They begin making smooth strokes up and down, painting as they look out the window.)

DUSTIN: When you paint rain, you have to move your hand gently. Yeah, like that. That's good.

TEDDY: As good as you?

DUSTIN: Better. You know how it feels, not just how it looks.

TEDDY: I'll show you how it feels.

DUSTIN: I was kidding when I said I wouldn't follow you out in the pouring rain. I would. We could go outside and play in the mud and climb trees. We could jump outside through the window too. It's only glass. You know how easy it is to break through glass. *(Lights out.)*

PETER PAN
by James Barrie

The Characters: Wendy (10) and *Peter (12)

This enchanting tale of the lost boys and their leader, Peter Pan, the little boy who doesn't want to grow up, has entertained readers and audiences for generations. Barrie's stage adaptation of his own book contains all of the memorable characters and episodes: Tinker Bell, the Darling family, Captain Hook and all of his pirates, and, of course, old Crock.

In the scene below, Wendy Darling awakens to discover an interesting stranger crying at the foot of her bed – it's Peter Pan.

*Editor's Note: Although this role is traditionally played by a female, the editors feel that it is outstanding material for both boys and girls to explore.

WENDY: *(Courteously.)* Boy, why are you crying?
(He jumps up, and crossing to the foot of the bed bows to her in the fairy way. Wendy, impressed, bows to him from the bed.)
PETER: What is your name?
WENDY: *(Well satisfied.)* Wendy Moira Angela Darling. What is yours?
PETER: *(Finding it lamentably brief.)* Peter Pan.
WENDY: Is that all?
PETER: *(Biting his lip.)* Yes.
WENDY: *(Politely.)* I am so sorry.
PETER: It doesn't matter.
WENDY: Where do you live?
PETER: Second to the right and then straight on till morning.
WENDY: What a funny address!
PETER: No, it isn't.
WENDY: I mean, is that what they put on the letters?
PETER: Don't get any letters.
WENDY: But your mother gets letters?
PETER: Don't have a mother.
WENDY: Peter!

(She leaps out of bed to put her arms round him, but he draws back; he does not know why, but he knows he must draw back.)

PETER: You mustn't touch me.

WENDY: Why?

PETER: No one must ever touch me.

WENDY: Why?

PETER: I don't know.

(He is never touched by anyone in the play.)

WENDY: No wonder you were crying.

PETER: I wasn't crying. But I can't get my shadow to stick on.

WENDY: It has come off! How awful. *(Looking at the spot where he had lain.)* Peter, you have been trying to stick it on with soap!

PETER: *(Snappily.)* Well then?

WENDY: It must be sewn on.

PETER: What is "sewn"?

WENDY: You are dreadfully ignorant.

PETER: No, I'm not.

WENDY: I will sew it on for you, my little man. But we must have more light. *(She touches something, and to his astonishment the room is illuminated.)* Sit here. I dare say it will hurt a little.

PETER: *(A recent remark of hers rankling.)* I never cry. *(She seems to attach the shadow. He tests the combination.)* It isn't quite itself yet.

WENDY: Perhaps I should have ironed it. *(It awakens and is as glad to be back with him as he to have it. He and his shadow dance together. He is showing off now. He crows like a cock. He would fly in order to impress Wendy further if he knew that there is anything unusual in that.)*

PETER: Wendy, look, look; oh the cleverness of me!

WENDY: You conceit; of course I did nothing!

PETER: You did a little.

WENDY: *(Wounded.)* A little! If I am no use I can at least withdraw. *(With one haughty leap she is again in bed with the sheet over her face. Popping on to the end of the bed the artful one appeals.)*

PETER: Wendy, don't withdraw. I can't help crowing, Wendy, when I'm pleased with myself. Wendy, one girl is worth more than twenty boys.

WENDY: *(Peeping over the sheet.)* You really think so, Peter?

PETER: Yes, I do.

WENDY: I think it's perfectly sweet of you, and I shall get up again.

(They sit together on the side of the bed.) I shall give you a kiss if you like.

PETER: Thank you. *(He holds out his hand.)*

WENDY: *(Aghast.)* Don't you know what a kiss is?

PETER: I shall know when you give it me. *(Not to hurt his feelings, she gives him her thimble.)* Now shall I give you a kiss?

WENDY: *(Primly.)* If you please. *(He pulls an acorn button off his person and bestows it on her. She is shocked but considerate.)* I will wear it on this chain round my neck. Peter, how old are you?

PETER: *(Blithely.)* I don't know, but quite young, Wendy. I ran away the day I was born.

WENDY: Ran away, why?

PETER: Because I heard father and mother talking of what I was to be when I became a man. I want always to be a little boy and to have fun; so I ran away to Kensington Gardens and lived a long time among the fairies.

WENDY: *(With great eyes.)* You know fairies, Peter!

PETER: *(Surprised that this should be a recommendation.)* Yes, but they are nearly all dead now. *(Baldly.)* You see, Wendy, when the first baby laughed for the first time, the laugh broke into a thousand pieces and they all went skipping about, and that was the beginning of fairies. And now when every new baby is born its first laugh becomes a fairy. So there ought to be one fairy for every boy or girl.

WENDY: *(Breathlessly.)* Ought to be? Isn't there?

PETER: Oh, no. Children know such a lot now. Soon they don't believe in fairies, and every time a child says "I don't believe in fairies" there is a fairy somewhere that falls down dead. *(He skips about heartlessly.)*

WENDY: Poor things!

PETER: *(To whom this statement recalls a forgotten friend.)* I can't think where she has gone. Tinker Bell, Tink, where are you?

WENDY: *(Thrilling.)* Peter, you don't mean to tell me that there is a fairy in this room!

PETER: *(Flitting about in search.)* She came with me. You don't hear anything, do you?

WENDY: I hear ...the only sound I hear is like a tinkle of bells.

PETER: That is the fairy language. I hear it too.

WENDY: It seems to come from over there.

PETER: *(With shameless glee.)* Wendy, I believe I shut her up in that drawer!

(He releases Tink, who darts about in a fury using language it is perhaps as well we don't understand.)

PETER: You needn't say that; I'm very sorry, but how could I know you were in the drawer?

WENDY: *(Her eyes dancing in pursuit of the delicious creature.)* Oh, Peter, if only she would stand still and let me see her!

PETER: *(Indifferently.)* They hardly ever stand still.

(To show that she can do even this Tink pauses between two ticks of the cuckoo clock.)

WENDY: I see her, the lovely! Where is she now?

PETER: She is behind the clock. Tink, this lady wishes you were her fairy. *(The answer comes immediately.)*

WENDY: What does she say?

PETER: She is not very polite. She says you are a great ugly girl, and that she is my fairy. You know, Tink, you can't be my fairy because I am a gentleman and you are a lady.

(Tink replies.)

WENDY: What did she say?

PETER: She said "You silly ass." She is quite a common girl, you know. She is called Tinker Bell because she mends the fairy pots and kettles.

WENDY: Where do you live now?

PETER: With the lost boys.

WENDY: Who are they?

PETER: They are the children who fall out of their prams when the nurse is looking the other way. If they are not claimed in seven days they are sent far away to Never Land. I'm captain.

WENDY: What fun it must be.

PETER: *(Craftily.)* Yes, but we are rather lonely. You see, Wendy, we have no female companionship.

WENDY: Are none of the other children girls?

PETER: Oh no; girls, you know, are much too clever to fall out of their prams.

WENDY: Peter, it is perfectly lovely the way you talk about girls. John there just despises us.

(Peter, for the first time, has a good look at John. He then neatly tumbles him out of bed.)

WENDY: You wicked! You are not captain here. *(She bends over her brother who is prone on the floor.)* After all he hasn't wakened, and you meant to be kind. *(Having now done her duty she forgets John, who blissfully sleeps on.)* Peter, you may give me a kiss.

PETER: *(Cynically.)* I thought you would want it back.

(He offers her the thimble.)

WENDY: *(Artfully.)* Oh dear, I didn't mean a kiss, Peter. I meant a thimble.

PETER: *(Only half placated.)* What is that?

WENDY: It is like this. *(She leans forward to give a demonstration, but something prevents the meeting of their faces.)*

PETER: *(Satisfied.)* Now shall I give you a thimble?

WENDY: If you please. *(Before he can even draw near she screams.)*

PETER: What is it?

WENDY: It was exactly as if someone were pulling my hair!

PETER: That must have been Tink. I never knew her so naughty before.

(Tink speaks. She is in the jug again.)

WENDY: What does she say?

PETER: She says she will do that every time I give you a thimble.

WENDY: But why?

PETER: *(Equally nonplussed.)* Why, Tink? *(He has to translate the answer.)* She said "You silly ass" again.

WENDY: She is very impertinent. *(They are sitting on the floor now.)* Peter, why did you come to our nursery window?

PETER: To try to hear stories. None of us know any stories.

WENDY: How perfectly awful!

PETER: Do you know why swallows build in the eaves of houses? It is to listen to the stories. Wendy, your mother was telling you such a lovely story.

WENDY: Which story was it?

PETER: About the prince, and he couldn't find the lady who wore the glass slipper.

WENDY: That was Cinderella. Peter, he found her and they were happy ever after.

PETER: I am glad. *(They have worked their way along the floor close to each other, but he now jumps up.)*

WENDY: Where are you going?

PETER: *(Already on his way to the window.)* To tell the other boys.

WENDY: Don't go, Peter. I know lots of stories. The stories I could tell to the boys!

PETER: *(Gleaming.)* Come on! We'll fly.

WENDY: Fly? You can fly!

(How he would like to rip those stories out of her; he is dangerous now.)

PETER: Wendy, come with me.

WENDY: Oh dear, we mustn't. Think of mother. Besides, I can't fly.

PETER: I'll teach you.

WENDY: How lovely to fly!

PETER: I'll teach you how to jump on the wind's back and then away we go. Wendy, when you are sleeping in your silly bed you might be flying about with me, saying funny things to the stars. There are mermaids, Wendy, with long tails. *(She just succeeds in remaining on the nursery floor.)* Wendy, how we should all respect you.

(At this she strikes her colours.)

WENDY: Of course it's awfully fas-cin-a-ting! Would you teach John and Michael to fly too?

PETER: *(Indifferently.)* If you like.

Roll Of Thunder Hear My Cry

Adapted for the stage by E. Shockley
From the novel by Mildred D. Taylor

The Characters: Cassie (12-14) Lillian Jean (12-14)

The story is set in Spokane County, Mississippi, 1934, a frightening time of conflict between race and culture. We see that the struggles faced by an entire race of people in the United States was a struggle embraced by young and old alike. No one is spared in the burning damage of racism. Cassie Logan is the daughter of Paul and Mary, who barely get by with Paul working their land and Mary teaching in the black-only school. Together with her brothers, Little Man and Stacey, Cassie grapples with a community that denies her her civil rights. She is not allowed to speak up when treated unfairly. Recently, Cassie has been the victim of harsh treatment in town. When she speaks in her own defense after being pushed by Lillian Jean, Lillian Jean's father pushes Cassie into the dirty street - threatening to beat her. Although her grandmother saves her from the beating, Cassie plots a revenge to get even with Lillian Jean. In the first scene, Cassie cleverly sets up a false-friendship to win allegiance with Lillian Jean in order to later spring her trap.

CASSIE: They just don't understand how things go, do they?

LILLIAN JEAN: Certainly not that towhead brother of mine. That's why daddy is always lighting into him.

CASSIE: Do tell.

LILLIAN JEAN: One time daddy couldn't find his strap so he picked up a log out the woodpile and clunked Jeremy up beside the head. Knocked him out cold.

CASSIE: No.

LILLIAN JEAN: Why, here we are at the crossroads already.

CASSIE: Isn't that a shame.

LILLIAN JEAN: It's as if we just flew here.

CASSIE: Here're your books and I'll meet you after school to tote 'em again.

LILLIAN JEAN: But you get out a whole half hour before Jefferson Davis.

CASSIE: You're the only white person I know nice enough to let me practice my place so I don't get into trouble next time I'm in town. That's worth waiting on, ain't it?

LILLIAN JEAN: Oh, Cassie Logan, you are just about the sweetest little nigra that ever was. Sure you can fetch my books and after Christmas I'll teach you how to behave right to your betters and you can listen to my secrets about beaus and such just like the nigra ladies in the picture shows.

CASSIE: I sure would like that, Miz Lillian Jean. Now you better hurry on to school before you're late.

LILLIAN JEAN: See you later.

CASSIE: See you later.

(Exit Lillian Jean.)

I sure hope I know what I'm getting in to.

In this second scene, Cassie has taken Lillian Jean (who is now convinced that Cassie is a true ally) to a remote and secluded section of the countryside.

CASSIE: Stacey sound just like Hammer or somebody telling T.J. that he was good as dead. Poor boy looked like he'd just been slapped with a brick too; but I ain't gonna be satisfied till I pull me some hair.

(Lillian Jean appears.)

LILLIAN JEAN: I just about gave up on you today.

CASSIE: I'm surprised you didn't, Miz Lillian, late as I am.

LILLIAN JEAN: Well, I just got so used to our visits till it wouldn't seem like the day was complete without one.

CASSIE: We have been doing this for what seem like forever, haven't we?

LILLIAN JEAN: Two months to the day.

CASSIE: Then we got to celebrate.

LILLIAN JEAN: Why Cassie, the idea.

CASSIE: Follow me.

LILLIAN JEAN: Where?

CASSIE: I want to show you a special spot I found. A place that only you and I will know about so then when you want to tell me about your Pa or your brothers or your beaus at school, we won't have to worry about nobody else hearing.

LILLIAN JEAN: Why if anybody was to hear half the things I tell you, Cassie, then I think I'd up and die.

CASSIE: I bet you would.

LILLIAN JEAN: That's why it's so wonderful having a little nigra confidant. I can tell you things that I could never tell any of my friends.

CASSIE: And you do your share of talking, Miz Lillian.

LILLIAN JEAN: Just wait till you hear what I told Joe Calvert about Suzanna Pemberton.

CASSIE: Calvert's the boy who you're sweet on, right?

LILLIAN JEAN: And Suzanna's the little fast thing that keeps showing him her panties every chance she gets.

CASSIE: Here we are.

LILLIAN JEAN: This is terribly secluded.

CASSIE: That's the point.

LILLIAN JEAN: Doesn't it make you feel just a mite uncomfortable being this far from everything?

CASSIE: No.

LILLIAN JEAN: Why, a body could scream to high heavens and no one's likely to hear her past the edge of this hollow.

CASSIE: That's exactly why I like it.

LILLIAN JEAN: Cassie Logan, you stop trying to spook me.

CASSIE: Or what?

LILLIAN JEAN: I beg your pardon?

CASSIE: Or what, Lillian Jean?

LILLIAN JEAN: You call me Miz Lillian Jean like you spozed to.

CASSIE: Make me.

LILLIAN JEAN: Have you lost your mind?

CASSIE: Yeah. Carrying your books done made me crazy in the head.

LILLIAN JEAN: You pick up my books this instant.

CASSIE: Tell your granny to pick 'em up.

LILLIAN JEAN: You mind me nigger, you hear!
(*Lillian slaps Cassie.*)

CASSIE: Thank you Miz Lillian Jean Simms...cause now that you done hit me first my Papa can't give me no whipping for what I'm about to do.

LILLIAN JEAN: You lay one finger on me, Cassandra Logan, and I'll tell my Pa.

CASSIE: Naw you won't. Not after you done told me all them secrets about R.W. and Melvin's stealing or your Pa half killing Jeremy on account of his being illegitimate or what about what you and that Calvert boy did in the cloak room on the night of the Christmas party?

LILLIAN JEAN: You wouldn't dare tell my daddy about that.

CASSIE: You speak on me and I'm gonna tell everything I know about you to everybody who needs to know it.

LILLIAN JEAN: But why, Cassie? I thought you were my little friend.

CASSIE: Come take your licking, child.
(They fight. Cassie ends up sitting on top of her.)
Now, you gonna 'pologize to me.

LILLIAN JEAN: I ain't gonna do no such thing.

CASSIE: Girl, you want me to snatch you bald?

LILLIAN JEAN: Ow!

CASSIE: You gonna 'pologize.

LILLIAN JEAN: 'Pologize for what?

CASSIE: For every mean, spiteful, snooty thing you ever done to me and ever gonna do to any negro for as long as your hard head got hair.

LILLIAN JEAN: I ain't gonna 'pologize to no nigra.
(Cassie pulls hair.)
Alright. Alright. I'm sorry.

CASSIE: I'm sorry Miz Cassandra Logan.

LILLIAN JEAN: Doggone your uppity...ow!

CASSIE: Say it!

LILLIAN JEAN: I'm sorry Miz Cassandra Logan.

CASSIE: Now git on home, girl.
(Lillian Jean starts to leave.)
And don't forget to tote your books.
(Exit Lillian Jean.)
The preacher say revenge ain't good for the soul, but it sure do make a body feel like singing out loud.
Roll of thunder
Hear my cry.
Lead me over...
(Black out. Thunder.)

ROOTS IN A PARCHED GROUND
by Horton Foote

The Characters: Horace (12) and Paul Horace Robedaux (adult)

Horace Robedaux lives with his mother, Corella; sister, Lily Dale, and grandparents, Mr. and Mrs. Thornton. Horace's father, Paul Horace Robedaux, has separated from his mother and lives with his family in the same town. Paul Horace is very ill, so ill in fact that he can no longer work. Young Horace struggles from a loss of a family, torn between the love he feels for his mother and father.

In this first scene, Horace gets a rare opportunity to visit his sick father.

*SPECIAL NOTE: You may wish to also read *Convicts* and *The Death of Papa*, part of the series of plays about Horace Robedaux also featured in this volume.

HORACE: Hello, Papa. How do you feel?

ROBEDAUX: Pretty well, thank you. How are you, Son?

HORACE: I'm just fine, Papa.

ROBEDAUX: Is it a pretty day out?

HORACE: Yes, Sir.

ROBEDAUX: Have you been fishing this afternoon?

HORACE: No, Sir. I'll go down later on and check on my lines.

ROBEDAUX: How's Lily Dale?

HORACE: She's fine.

ROBEDAUX: And your mother?

HORACE: She's fine.

ROBEDAUX: Is she still in Houston?

HORACE: Yes, Sir. She's come home now on a visit, though. Aunt Mary is here too. They were all over there this afternoon together, singing, but Grandma said it was disturbing you so I asked them to stop it.

ROBEDAUX: It certainly wasn't disturbing me. You tell them to sing all they want to.

HORACE: Yes, Sir.

ROBEDAUX: Does your mother like Houston?

HORACE: Yes, Sir. I guess so.

ROBEDAUX: Do you think you and Lily Dale will ever go live with her in Houston?

HORACE: I don't know, Sir. Mama thinks I should live with Grandpa because he can make me behave.

ROBEDAUX: Did you go to school today?

HORACE: No, Sir.

ROBEDAUX: Did you go any this week?

HORACE: No, Sir.

ROBEDAUX: You don't like school?

HORACE: No, Sir.

ROBEDAUX: Why?

HORACE: I just don't. I'm not smart.

ROBEDAUX: Do you study?

HORACE: Sometimes.

ROBEDAUX: Bring your books over here tomorrow.

HORACE: Yes, Sir. *(Pause.)* What for?

ROBEDAUX: I just want to see what you know.

HORACE: I don't know anything.

ROBEDAUX: Yes, you do.

HORACE: No, I don't. I'm dumb.

ROBEDAUX: You're not dumb, Horace. You don't study.

HORACE: I'm dumb.

ROBEDAUX: Who says so?

HORACE: My teacher.

ROBEDAUX: Who is your teacher?

HORACE: Miss Phillips.

ROBEDAUX: Well, you're not dumb.

HORACE: Yes, I am.

(Robedaux closes his eyes. Pause.)

ROBEDAUX: I want you to bring your books over here every day. If I can't work with you, your Uncle Terrence can.

HORACE: He reads Latin and Greek, don't he?

ROBEDAUX: Doesn't he.

HORACE: Doesn't he?

ROBEDAUX: Yes.

HORACE: Are you a lawyer?

ROBEDAUX: Yes.

HORACE: You and Mr. John Howard are partners? His two children were burned up in a fire, weren't they?

ROBEDAUX: Yes.

HORACE: They say that has affected his wife's mind. She never leaves the house. Did you ever see her?

ROBEDAUX: Yes.

HORACE: Was she pretty?

ROBEDAUX: Yes.

HORACE: Did you ever know his children?

ROBEDAUX: Yes.

HORACE: How long ago was the fire?

ROBEDAUX: Ten years ago.

The Characters: Horace (12) and Lloyd (12)

In this second scene, Horace's father has passed away this very day and Horace's friend, Lloyd, finds him fishing by the river.

LLOYD: Did you have any luck?

HORACE: No...

LLOYD: Are you gonna fish any more?

HORACE: No, I've got to go home now.

LLOYD: Did you go to school today?

HORACE: No.

LLOYD: Did you quit school?

HORACE: No, I just didn't feel like going.

LLOYD: If I didn't go to school every day, I'd get it. You got any chewing tobacco?

HORACE: No.

LLOYD: Let's go down to the alley and get some empty whiskey bottles to sell so we can buy some tobacco.

HORACE: I can't.

LLOYD: Why?

HORACE: I have to go home.

LLOYD: Why?

HORACE: My papa died.

LLOYD: He died? When?

HORACE: Just awhile ago.

LLOYD: I bet my father is going to be one of the pallbearers, don't you? They're good friends. They always ask your good friends to be your pallbearers.

In this scene, Horace and Lloyd meet on the day that Horace's mother and sister return from Houston, where they moved in search of work and lodging after the father passed away. His mother promised to bring Horace later, however, she has married a Houston railroad worker, Mr. Davenport, and it now looks questionable where Horace will fit into this new family.

(The riverbank. Horace is there stretched out on his back, smoking a pipe. Lloyd comes in. In the distance we can hear the aunts singing.)

LLOYD: There's singing over at your house. *(He takes out a pipe too, and begins to smoke.)* Why aren't you up there with the rest?

HORACE: Too noisy. Too many people. I like it down here where it's quiet.

LLOYD: Did you meet your new daddy? *(Horace nods his head yes.)* What's his name?

HORACE: Mr. Davenport.

LLOYD: What's his first name?

HORACE: Pete.

LLOYD: What do you call him?

HORACE: Mr. Davenport.

LLOYD: Mr. Davenport?

HORACE: Yes.

LLOYD: I guess that's because you're not used to him. *(Pause.)* Do you think you'll ever call him anything else?

HORACE: Nope.

LLOYD: My mama says she bets you'll go live with them now.

HORACE: Nope. They want me to, but I won't go.

LLOYD: Why? I'd like to live in Houston.

HORACE: I wouldn't. They say if I do go, I'd have to go to school, and I'm through with school.

LLOYD: You're not going back to school?

HORACE: Nope.

LLOYD: What are you going to do?

HORACE: Going out to the Gautier plantation with my uncle and work in the store.

LLOYD: How much will he pay you?

HORACE: My grub, all the tobacco I want, and four bits a week.

LLOYD: You're on your own now.

HORACE: I'm on my own.

LLOYD: See the lanterns down at the bottom? They're looking for Mr. Ritter. They think he may have died down there. Mr. John Howard died.

HORACE: I know.

LLOYD: They're not going to bury him here.

HORACE: I heard.

LLOYD: Did you go to your daddy's funeral?

HORACE: No. I've never been to a funeral.

LLOYD: Neither have I. Maybe we can go to Mr. Ritter's funeral, if they find him.

(Pause. They listen to the music.)

Do all your aunts sing?

HORACE: Yes.

LLOYD: And they all play musical instruments?

HORACE: Yes.

LLOYD: Do you play anything?

HORACE: No.

LLOYD: Last time I talked to you, you were going on about studying law in Houston.

HORACE: I've changed my mind. I wouldn't care for a city, I decided. I'd miss my fishing.

LLOYD: Aren't you going to study law here?

HORACE: No.

LLOYD: You change your mind a lot. Two months ago you were going on about studying law in Mr. John Howard's law office.

HORACE: Mr. John Howard is dead.

LLOYD: I know that. What do you think we were talking about just a minute ago? He's not the only lawyer in the world, you know. Mr. George Tyler is a lawyer. You could study law in his office.

HORACE: Mr. George Tyler has a son. He'll be studying law in his office. Anyway, I've changed my mind about all that.

LLOYD: You have?

HORACE: I certainly have. Lawyers are a dime a dozen, you know. There's no future in it.

LLOYD: I reckon not.

HORACE: No future at all. How much do tombstones cost? Do you know?

LLOYD: About a hundred dollars, I reckon. Why?

HORACE: I thought I might save my money and buy one.

LLOYD: What for?

HORACE: To put on my daddy's grave.

LLOYD: Take you a long time to save a hundred dollars.
[*(Two men come in.)*

FIRST MAN: Boys, you all haven't seen anything strange while you've been back here?

LLOYD: What you mean, strange?

FIRST MAN: You haven't seen an old man's body of any kind?

LLOYD: No, Sir. If we had, we would have reported it.

FIRST MAN: Keep your eyes open. Old man Ritter's lost or dead down here, we're afraid.]

LLOYD: I'm going home. Are you coming?

HORACE: I guess so.

A ROSEN BY ANY OTHER NAME
by Israel Horovitz

The Characters: Fern (13) and Stanley (13)

Stanley Rosen is at the age where Jewish boys pass into manhood – he is preparing for his bar mitzvah. He and his family live in Ontario, Canada, and it is the start of the Second World War. Because of the anti-Jewish sentiments in Europe, Stanley's father thinks they should change their name from Rosen to Royal. Stanley feels differently, however. He is proud to be a Rosen and proud to become a man as all Jewish men do, by having his bar mitzvah. On top of this struggle, Stanley and his enemy, Irving Yanover, are fighting over the same girl, a gentile named Fern. Here are two telephone conversations between Stanley and Fern.

*SPECIAL NOTE: You may wish to also read *Today I am a Fountain Pen,* also featured in this volume.

(Lights fade up on Fern in her bedroom. She also talks on telephone, while polishing nails.)

FERN: Did I not tell you to never call after eight? What is the *matter* with you?

STANLEY: I promised to call you at six and forgot…we're having a crisis in our house…

FERN: There's no excuse for calling me after eight…

STANLEY: I thought you'd be upset if I didn't call at all…

FERN: Why should I be?

STANLEY: Because we talk every night. Because we never miss a night…

FERN: Miss all the nights you want. I'd never notice.

STANLEY: Fern, I have to ask you a really personal question…
Please.

FERN: Okay, but make it snappy…

STANLEY: Do you think kids at school hate me because I'm Jewish?

FERN: That's not why the kids at school hate you, Stanley.

STANLEY: Oh, that's great. I'm so relieved.

FERN: I'm going to hang up now, Stanley…

STANLEY: Sure, I understand. Swell talking to you, Fern…I'll see
you in my dreams.

FERN: That's a grotesque idea, Stanley.

STANLEY: Will you dream of me, Fern?

FERN: Of course not!

STANLEY: Good night, Fern…

FERN: Good night, Stanley…

---

*(Fern's light fades up. She is in her window, holding inevitable
phone. Stanley turns and talks to Fern, as if on telephone.)*

FERN: What, Stanley? What could be so important, Stanley? It's so
late! I'll get killed for this!

STANLEY: Fern, please, please…

FERN: Well, whhhhhattt?

STANLEY: Please, Fern! What I have to ask is very…difficult…and
when you're in a snit, I don't think I can ask it…

FERN: I am not in a snit, Stanley Rosen! For your information, your
friend Irving Yanover keeps calling me and calling me. He's
probably rung this telephone fifteen times tonight and my parents
are furious…

STANLEY: What the hell is Yanover calling you about?

FERN: I think that's my personal business, don't you? If you want to
ask me a question, Stanley, please do it *now!*

STANLEY: *(Quietly; quickly.)* If I were to pick you up now at your
house, would you run away with me and get married and live in
Ottawa?

FERN: No.

STANLEY: Vancouver?

FERN: No.

STANLEY: How about Jasper? It's beautiful.

FERN: No.

STANLEY: I see. You won't marry me?

FERN: No, Stanley, I won't.

STANLEY: Will you just run away with me?

FERN: No.

STANLEY: If I were to run away and then send for you, would you
follow me later?

FERN: No.

STANLEY: Do you love me more than words can say?

FERN: No.

STANLEY: Oh, God! Fern, let me just get this straight, you won't run away with me?...

FERN: No.

STANLEY: You won't follow me, or marry me?

FERN: No, no!

STANLEY: Are you in love with Irving Yanover?

FERN: Oh, my God, Stanley, don't be *disgusting!*

STANLEY: *(Giggles.)* Great talking with you, Fern...

THE SECRET GARDEN
Musical Book and Lyrics by Marsha Norman
based on the novel by Frances Hodgson Burnett

The Characters: Mary (10) and Colin (10)

After young Mary Lennox's mother and father die from cholera in India, she is sent to live at the large manor home of her Uncle Archibald Craven in England. The manor is filled with "Dreamers," the spirits of people who have died. There is a sadness in the halls and the decaying gardens, particularly a special, secret, garden that holds the promise of hope and new happiness. The sadness has for ten years been a part of the manor, for it was ten years ago that Archibald's lovely wife, Lily, died giving birth to their only son, Colin. Out of fear that Colin would be physically deformed like his father (who has a hunchback) and not survive, he has been protected and sheltered from the outside world.

In this first scene, Mary discovers Colin for the first time in his room, propped up on his bed.

*SPECIAL NOTE: Characters who appear in the stage directions are some of the "Dreamers," ghostly spirits of family members and servants who have died.

(Colin's room. A ghostly form lying on a bed, screaming. Mary is terrified.)

COLIN: Get out!

MARY: Who are *you?*

COLIN: Who are *you?* Are you a ghost?

MARY: No I am not. I am Mary Lennox. Mr. Craven is my uncle.

COLIN: How do I know you're not a ghost?

MARY: I'll pinch you if you like. That will show you how real I am. Who are you?

COLIN: I am Colin. Mr. Craven is my *father.* I see no one and no one sees me. Including my father. I am going to die.

MARY: How do you know?

COLIN: Because I hear everybody whispering about it. If I live, I may be a hunchback, but I shan't live.

MARY: Well, I've seen lots of dead people, and you don't look like any of them.

COLIN: Dead people! Where did you *come* from?

MARY: From India. My parents died there of the cholera. But I don't know what happened to them after that. Perhaps they burned them.

COLIN: My mother died too. When I was born. That's why my father hates me.

MARY: He hates the garden too.

COLIN: What garden?

(Mary wishes she hadn't said anything about the garden.)

MARY: Just a garden your mother liked. Have you always been in this bed?

COLIN: Sometimes I have been taken to places at the seaside, but I won't stay because people stare at me. And one time a grand doctor came from London, and said to take off this iron thing Dr. Craven made me wear and keep me out in the fresh air. But I hate fresh air, and I won't be taken out.

MARY: If you don't like people to see you, do you want me to go away?

COLIN: Yes, but I want you to come back first thing tomorrow morning and tell me all about India. In the books my father sends me, I've read that elephants can swim. Have you ever seen them swim? They seem too altogether large to be swimmers, unless perhaps they use their ears to –

MARY: I can't come talk to you in the morning. I have to go outside and look for something with Dickon.

COLIN: Who's Dickon?

MARY: He's Martha's brother. He's my friend.

(Suddenly, Colin's despotic temperament flares.)

COLIN: If you go outside with that Dickon instead of coming here to talk to me, I'll send him away.

MARY: You *can't* send Dickon away!

COLIN: I can do whatever I want. If I were to live, this entire place would belong to me someday. And they *all* know that.

MARY: You little Rajah! If you send Dickon away, I'll never come into this room again.

COLIN: I'll make you. They'll drag you in here.

MARY: I won't even look at you. I'll stare at the floor.

COLIN: You are a selfish thing.

MARY: You're more selfish than I am. You're the most selfish boy I ever saw.

COLIN: I'm selfish because I'm dying.

MARY: You just say that to make people feel sorry for you. If you were a nice boy it might be true, but you're too nasty to die! *(Mary turns and stomps away toward the door. The Ayah appears.)*

COLIN: No, please don't go. *(She stops. Her Ayah hums an Indian lullaby.)*

COLIN: It's just that the storm scares me so that if I went to sleep, I know I'd have such terrible dreams...

MARY: But if you keep crying...

COLIN: ...or if I did sleep, I might not wake up.

MARY: Would you like me to stay with you until you fall asleep?

COLIN: I should like that very much.

MARY: Then close your eyes, and I will do what my Ayah used to do in India. I will pat your hand and stroke it and sing something quite low.

COLIN: Do you have bad dreams, too?

MARY: Not always. Sometimes I dream about tea parties, but I never know who anybody is at the parties. Or since I've been here, whenever I see my father in a dream, he's a hunchback like your father, and sometimes my Ayah has my mother's face...

In this second scene, Mary challenges Colin to stop throwing tantrums and get on with his life.

MARY: Colin Craven, you stop that screaming!

COLIN: Get away from me!

MARY: I hate you! Everybody hates you! You will scream yourself to death in a minute and I wish you would!

COLIN: Get out of my house!

MARY: I won't! You stop!

COLIN: I can't stop! I felt a lump on my back. I'm going to die!

MARY: There is nothing the matter with your horrid back!

COLIN: I'm going to have a hunch on my back like my father and die!

MARY: Martha! Come here and show me his back this minute.

[**MARTHA:** I can't, Mary. He won't let me.]

COLIN: Show her the lump!

(Martha pulls aside Colin's covers and bedclothes.)

COLIN: Now feel it!

(Mary feels his back.)

COLIN: There!

MARY: Where?

COLIN: Right there!

MARY: No! There's not a single lump there. Except backbone lumps and they're supposed to be there. *(She turns her own back to him.)* See. I have them too.

(Mary grabs his hand and puts it on her back. And then places his hand on his own back for comparison.)

MARY: See? There's no lump.

COLIN: *(Quietly.)* It's not there.

MARY: No, it's not.

(He sits up a little straighter. Looking slightly pleased.)

COLIN: It's not there.

MARY: You were just mad at me for not coming back when I said I would.

(He doesn't answer.)

MARY: Weren't you?

COLIN: Maybe.

MARY: *(Calmly.)* You were and you know it.

[**MARTHA:** I'll leave you two alone, I think. *(She leaves.)*]

(Mary opens a music box, determined not to speak to him until he apologizes.)

MARY: This is nice.

(Colin relents.)

COLIN: I'm sorry I said all those things about sending Dickon away. I was just so angry when you wanted to be with him instead of me. And then when you didn't come back like you said you would –

MARY: I was always coming back, Colin. I'm as lonely as you are. I was just late, that's all. It just took me longer than I thought because…*(She stops.)*

COLIN: Because what?

(Mary takes a moment.)

MARY: Will you promise not to tell if I tell you?

COLIN: I never had a secret before, except that I wasn't going to grow up.

MARY: I found your mother's garden.

COLIN: Do you mean a secret garden? I've dreamed about a secret garden.

MARY: It's been locked up out there, just like you've been locked up in here, for ten years. Because your father doesn't want anybody in it. Only I found the key. And the other night, after Dr. Craven and Mrs. Medlock found us here together, I ran out into the storm, and found the door. And now Dickon and I are working on it every day, and you can come too and –

COLIN: What does it look like?

MARY: Well, right now, there's this tangle of vines all over everything because nobody's been taking care of it, but Dickon says if we cut away all the dead wood, there'll be fountains of roses by summer.

COLIN: I never wanted to see anything like I want to see that garden.

MARY: You *must see it*. But they must never know where we're going or Ben says that Dr. Craven will send me away.

COLIN: No, Mary.

MARY: *(Going on.)* Maybe William can take you outside in your wheelchair, and leave us at the front steps. And then, when nobody's looking, Dickon could push you through the maze to the garden.

COLIN: I can't go outside, Mary. I'll take a chill if I go. I'll get even worse.

MARY: No you won't. You'll feel better.

COLIN: I can't, Mary. I'm afraid.
(And then Mary sees, in a shaft of light, the two officers who found her in India.)

COLIN: I've been in this bed for so long. And I don't want to die.

[LIEUTENANT WRIGHT: Just one blacksnake and this girl.

MAJOR HOLMES: I'm afraid there's no one left. Sorry, Miss.]
(Mary turns back to Colin.)

COLIN: I want to grow up, Mary. So I can't get sick. *(He pauses.)* I'd like to see the garden, really I would. But I can't.
(Lieutenant Wright and Major Holmes exit.)

MARY: All right, then. We'll just keep working on it till you're *ready* to see it. And whenever that is, you just tell me, and I'll get William to –

COLIN: You must come back tomorrow afternoon after you're through working, and have supper with me and tell me

everything you've done.
MARY: I'd like that. Good night, then.
COLIN: Good night, Mary.
   (*Mary leaves, Colin looks out the window.*)

SISTER MARY IGNATIUS EXPLAINS IT ALL FOR YOU
by Christopher Durang

The Characters: Sister Mary (adult) and Thomas (7)

Durang's rather disturbing yet funny play centers around a teaching nun, Sister Mary Ignatius, who has prepared a lecture concerning the consequences of committing any one of the various forms of sin. During the course of the lecture, she is confronted with several of her former students, each of whom feels betrayed by the lessons Sister Mary has taught. In the end, Sister Mary has to shed some blood in order to get her point across.

Below, Sister Mary is questioning one of her current and favorite pupils, Thomas, who can quote the Ten Commandments on cue.

SISTER: Thomas, how can we best keep from going to hell?

THOMAS: By not committing a mortal sin, by keeping close to the sacraments, especially going to confession and receiving communion, and by obeying our parents.

(She gives him a cookie.)

SISTER: Good boy. Do you love our Lord, Thomas?

THOMAS: Yes, Sister.

SISTER: How much?

THOMAS: This much. *(Holds arms out wide.)*

SISTER: Well, that's very nice, but Christ loves us an infinite amount. How do we know that, Thomas?

THOMAS: Because you tell us.

SISTER: That's right. And by His actions. He died on the cross for us to make up for our sins. Wasn't that nice of Him?

THOMAS: Very nice.

SISTER: And shouldn't we be grateful?

THOMAS: Yes, we should

SISTER: That's right. We should. *(Gives him a cookie.)* How do you spell cookie?

THOMAS: C-O-O-K-I-E.

SISTER: Very good. *(Gives him a cookie.)* Mary has had an argument with her parents and has shot and killed them. Is that a venial sin or a mortal sin?

THOMAS: That's a mortal sin.

SISTER: If she dies with this mortal sin on her soul, will she go to heaven or to hell?

THOMAS: She will go to hell.

SISTER: Very good. How do you spell ecumenical?

THOMAS: *(Sounding it out.)* Eck – E-C-K; you - U; men – M-E-N; ical – I-C-K-L-E.

SISTER: Very good. *(Gives him a cookie.)* What's two plus two?

THOMAS: Four.

SISTER: What's one and one and one and one and one and one and one and one and one?

THOMAS: Nine.

SISTER: Very good. *(Gives him a cookie.)* Because she is afraid to show her parents her bad report card, Susan goes to the top of a tall building and jumps off. Is this a venial sin or a mortal sin?

THOMAS: Mortal sin.

SISTER: And where will she go?

THOMAS: Hell.

SISTER: Sit on my lap.

(He does.)

Would you like to keep your pretty soprano voice forever?

THOMAS: Yes, Sister.

SISTER: Well, we'll see what we can do about it. *(Sings.)*

> Cookies in the morning,
> Cookies in the evening,
> Cookies in the summertime,
> Be my little cookie,
> And love me all the time.

God, I've done so much talking, I've got to rest my voice some. Here, you take care of some of these questions, Thomas, while I rest, all right, dear? *(She hands him the file cards.)*

THOMAS: Yes, Sister. *(Reads.)* How do we know there is a God? We know that there is a God because the Church tells us so. And also because everything has a primary cause. Dinner is put on the table because the primary cause, our mother, has put it in the oven and cooked it. *(Reads.)* If God is all powerful, why does He allow evil? *(Skips that one; next one.)* What does God look like? God looks like an old man, a young man, and a small white dove.

THE SKIN OF OUR TEETH
by Thornton Wilder

The Characters: Henry (14) and Antrobus (adult)

This is a story of survival. The Antrobus family survives just about
every sort of calamity thinkable, from war to plagues, the ice age, and
economic ruin. But they *do* survive. Part of the charm of this play is
that through it all, struggle after struggle, the Antrobus family is like
all families, human. Here young Henry has a serious discussion with
his father.

*(Enter Antrobus, his arms full of bundles, chewing the end of a
carrot. He has a slight limp. Over the suit of Act I he is wearing
an overcoat too long for him, its skirts trailing on the ground. He
lets his bundles fall and stands looking about. Presently his
attention is fixed on Henry, whose words grow clearer.)*

HENRY: All right! What have you got to lose? What have they done
for us? That's right – nothing. Tear everything down. I don't care
what you smash. We'll begin again and we'll show 'em.
*(Antrobus takes out his revolver and holds it pointing downwards.
With his back towards the audience he moves toward the
footlights. Henry's voice grows louder and he wakes with a start.
They stare at one another. Then Henry sits up quickly. Throughout
the following scene Henry is played, not as a misunderstood or
misguided young man, but as a representation of strong
unreconciled evil.)*

HENRY: All right! Do something.*(Pause.)* Don't think I'm afraid of
you, either. All right, do what you were going to do. Do it.
(Furiously.) Shoot me, I tell you. You don't have to think I'm any
relation of yours. I haven't got any father or any mother, or
brothers or sisters. And I don't want any. And what's more I
haven't got anybody over me; and I never will have. I'm alone,
and that's all I want to be: alone. So you can shoot me.

ANTROBUS: You're the last person I wanted to see. The sight of
you dries up all my plans and hopes. I wish I were back at war
still, because it's easier to fight you than to live with you. War's a
pleasure – do you hear me? – War's a pleasure compared to what

faces us now: trying to build up a peacetime with you in the middle of it. *(Antrobus walks up to the window.)*

HENRY: I'm not going to be a part of any peacetime of yours. I'm going a long way from here and make my own world that's fit for a man to live in. Where a man can be free, and have a chance, and do what he wants to do in his own way.

ANTROBUS: *(His attention arrested; thoughtfully. He throws the gun out of the window and turns with hope.)* ...Henry, let's try again.

HENRY: Try what? Living *here?* – Speaking polite downstairs to all the old men like you? Standing like a sheep at the street corner until the red light turns to green? Being a good boy and a good sheep, like all the stinking ideas you get out of your books? Oh, no. I'll make a world, and I'll show you.

ANTROBUS: *(Hard.)* How can you make a world for people to live in, unless you've first put order in yourself? Mark my words: I shall continue fighting you until my last breath as long as you mix up your idea of liberty with your idea of hogging everything for yourself. I shall have no pity on you. I shall pursue you to the far corners of the earth. You and I want the same thing; but until you think of it as something that everyone has a right to, you are my deadly enemy and I will destroy you. – I hear your mother's voice in the kitchen. Have you seen her?

HENRY: I have no mother. Get it into your head. I don't belong here. I have nothing to do here. I have no home.

ANTROBUS: Then why did you come here? With the whole world to choose from, why did you come to this one place: 216 Cedar Street, Excelsior, New Jersey...Well?

HENRY: What if I did? What if I wanted to look at it once more, to see if –

ANTROBUS: Oh, you're related, all right – When your mother comes in you must behave yourself. Do you hear me?

HENRY: *(Wildly.)* What is this? – *must behave* yourself. Don't say *must* to me.

ANTROBUS: Quiet!

(Enter Mrs. Antrobus and Sabina.)

HENRY: Nobody can say *must* to me. All my life everybody's been crossing me – everybody, everything, all of you. I'm going to be free, even if I have to kill half the world for it. Right now, too. Let me get my hands on his throat. I'll show him.

TO KILL A MOCKINGBIRD
Screenplay by Horton Foote
Based on the novel by Harper Lee

The Characters: Jem (10) and Scout (6)

Horton Foote's Academy Award-winning screen adaptation of the classic novel by Harper Lee presents this story of growing up, right and wrong, and the agony and ignorance of discrimination within a dramatic framework. Jem and Scout live with their father, Atticus, a widower, who is defending a black man he believes is wrongly accused of a terrible crime. The town is in hysterics and threats have been made toward the family. No one seems to be behind Atticus in his decision to defend this man. In this scene, Jem has escorted his young sister, Scout, to the Halloween pageant at school. Scout is costumed as a ham. It is very late. Most everyone has already left school.

*SPECIAL NOTE: The year is 1932 and the place is Maycomb, Alabama, a troubled time for race relations in America.

(Exterior: Schoolhouse. Night. The carriages and cars are now gone. Jem is seated on the steps of the schoolhouse. He gets up, walks up the steps to open the door, and looks inside.)

JEM: Scout.

SCOUT: *(Off camera.)* Yeah.

JEM: Will you come on. Everybody's gone.

SCOUT: *(Off camera.)* I can't go home like this.

JEM: Well, I'm goin'. It's almost ten o'clock and Atticus will be waitin' for us. *(He turns and comes down the steps.)*

SCOUT: *(Off camera.)* All right. I'm comin'. *(He turns and looks as Scout comes out of the door with her ham costume on.)* But I feel like a fool walkin' home like this.

JEM: Well, it's not my fault that you lost your dress.

SCOUT: I didn't lose it. Just can't find it.

(She comes down the steps to Jem.)

JEM: Where are your shoes?

SCOUT: Can't find them either.

JEM: You can get 'em tomorrow.

SCOUT: But tomorrow is Sunday.

JEM: You can get the janitor to let you in. Come on.
(Moving shot: They walk into the wooded area. Jem stoops down and picks up sticks and hits trees with them as they walk along. It is black dark out there.)

JEM: Here, Scout, let me hold onto you before you break your neck. *(Takes her hand as they walk.)*

SCOUT: Jem, you don't have to hold me.

JEM: Sshhhh.

SCOUT: What's the matter?

JEM: Hush a minute, Scout. *(Moves and looks to his right.)* Thought I heard somethin'. Ah, come on. *(They go about five paces when he makes her stop again.)* Wait.

SCOUT: Jem, are you tryin' to scare me?

JEM: Sshhh. *(There is stillness except for the breathing of the children. Far away a dog howls.)*

SCOUT: You know I'm too old.

JEM: Be quiet.

SCOUT: I heard an old dog then.

JEM: It's not that. I hear it when we're walking along. When we stop, I don't hear it any more.

SCOUT: You hear my costume rustlin'. Halloween's got you. *(Moves and then stops.)* I hear it now. *(The two of them stand still and listen.)* I'll bet it's just old Cecil Jacobs tryin' to scare us. *(She yells.)* Cecil Jacobs is a big wet hen.
(There is not a sound except the word "hen" reverberating.)

JEM: Come on.
(Scout and Jem start walking. Jem looks frightened. He holds his hand on Scout's head, covered by the ham costume. More than a rustle is heard now. Footsteps are heard, as if someone were walking behind them in heavy shoes. Jem presses Scout's head. They stop to listen. They can hear someone running toward them.)

JEM: Run, Scout!
(She takes a big step and she reels; she can't keep her balance in the dark. A form descends on her and grabs her, and she falls to the ground and rolls. From nearby, she can hear scuffling, kicking sounds, sounds of shoes and flesh scraping dirt and root. Jem rolls against her and is up like lightning, pulling Scout with him, but she is so entangled by the costume they can't get very far.)

JEM: Run, Scout!

TODAY, I AM A FOUNTAIN PEN
by Israel Horovitz

The Characters: Irving (10) and Annie (15)

Irving Yanover is a ten-year-old piano prodigy and an extremely outspoken young man. The time is 1941, the place is Ontario, Canada. Like the other two plays in this trilogy (*A Rosen by Any Other Name* and *The Chopin Playoffs*), this play deals with a struggle for what tradition and family values dictate and what, in reality, is the truth in life. Irving argues with his parents over many things, especially eating kosher when he knows that they sometimes don't. It is also a story of a young Ukrainian girl, Annie, who is working for Irving's family and who is in love with a man that her family will not accept.

In this first scene, Irving opens up to Annie about the differences in their upbringing.

*SPECIAL NOTE: You may wish to also read *A Rosen by Any Other Name*, also featured in this volume.

(Lights up in the bedroom. Irving is lying atop his bed; Annie is arranging things on her dresser top.)

IRVING: Do you hate sharing a bedroom?

ANNIE: I'm used to sharing a *bed*.

IRVING: I guess that's okay if the bed's big.

ANNIE: It was pretty big...

IRVING: My mother and father's bed is *great*. Maybe we could share that sometime.

ANNIE: *(Looks at Irving: smiles.)* Do you do well in school?

IRVING: If I didn't, I'd be dead. You'd have the whole bedroom to yourself. I got seven "Excellents" and one "Very Good"... *(Pauses in disgust.)* Stanley Rosen got eight "Excellents."

ANNIE: You really hate him, huh?

IRVING: You'll see. When you meet him, you'll hate him too. He's a twerp and a jerk.

ANNIE: Oh, yuh. I hate twerps and jerks. *(Irving giggles approvingly.)*

IRVING: Hey, maybe I could get him here for supper with his parents and you could slip some poison onto his brisket. *(Pauses.)* I'm planning to murder Stanley Rosen.

ANNIE: I can see why. Eight excellents. What a twerp!

IRVING: *(Pleased.)* Do Ukrainians really eat weird things?

ANNE: What kind of weird things?

IRVING: Oh, well...like cabbage?

ANNIE: Cabbage isn't weird.

IRVING: How about bacon?

ANNIE: You think bacon is weird?

IRVING: I think bacon is wonderful, but it is totally illegal for Jews. Pig food.

ANNIE: Pig food?

IRVING: Pig food.

ANNIE: Pigs eat bacon?

IRVING: Pigs *are* bacon.

ANNIE: Right. Well, if cabbage and bacon is weird food, then I guess Ukrainians eat weird food...*(Annie reties the twine around her dilapidated suitcase.)*

IRVING: How come you had twine tied around your suitcase? When you first came here I noticed your suitcase was tied together with twine...but, when you opened it, there wasn't much in there...to fall out, I mean...

ANNIE: *(Looks at Irving; pauses.)* Better safe than sorry, I guess...

IRVING: How come you brought so little? The last girl needed two whole drawers, she had so much stuff.

ANNIE: I guess she was fancy.

IRVING: Nawww. She wasn't fancy. I heard my mother talking to my father about her, after she quit. She forgot some of her underwear and my mother said it was really filthy...*(Pauses.)* Do you think I'm really funny?

ANNIE: When I first got here I noticed your big eyes, right away, and I thought, "What big eyes this little boy has!"...and then I got to hear your big mouth, and I thought "What a big mouth for a little boy!" Now I've found out that you also have inordinately big ears – they hear *every*thing, right! So, I guess it stands to reason that you've gotta have the big head you've got...'cause you are really the Big Head of all time!...but you've gotta have a big head, right? 'cause it's got to lug all that other BIG STUFF AROUND!

IRVING: *(Looks up to Heaven.)* WHY MEEE? *(Blackout.)*

In this second scene, Irving discovers that Annie has a boyfriend.

IRVING: I can't believe you got permission! Did you have to lie?

ANNIE: I don't lie.

IRVING: Never?

ANNIE: Never. *(And with that, Annie leans over and switches out the bed light between them. Lights out. There is a pause. Annie switches light on again. Irving is startled.)* Irving?

IRVING: What?

ANNIE: I did lie a little.

IRVING: I was worried, 'cause I lie a lot...all the time! What did you lie a little about?

ANNIE: Pete Lisanti...

IRVING: Who's Pete Lisanti?

ANNIE: My boyfriend. He's going to the movie with us...

IRVING: *(Not the best news he's ever heard.)* He is?

ANNIE: I left that part out with your father...

IRVING: With me, too...

ANNIE: Is it okay?

IRVING: I guess. If he's *your* boyfriend, he's my boyfriend too...

ANNIE: My parents would kill me if they found out...

IRVING: Why?

ANNIE: They made me promise I wouldn't go out with him...

IRVING: You're going to break your promise?

ANNIE: Well, yuh...sometimes you get pushed into making promises you really never want to make in the first place...

IRVING: Sure, well, *sure.* But a promise is a promise...*(Pete appears on stage, downstage of Annie and Irving, in the shadows. N.B.: room will soon become the cinema. Neither Annie nor Irving acknowledges Pete's presence, as yet.)*

ANNIE: It's different. Pete's my boyfriend...

IRVING: I guess.

ANNIE: I mean really my *boyfriend. (Pete steps upstage to Annie, touches her cheek with his hand. She doesn't turn, but, instead, reaches up and touches his hand on her cheek.)*

IRVING: You mean *dates!*

ANNIE: Dates. Dances...long walks...

IRVING: I know about those things...

ANNIE: Pete's a genius.

IRVING: Pete's a genius?

ANNIE: At hockey. He played for Tech until he graduated last year. His line was the best, two years straight, and he was the highest scorer, too...

IRVING: Did he go to the university?

ANNIE: Nooo, silly. He works nights at Algoma Steel, and he practices and plays during the daytime. He starts for the James Street Aces...He's the youngest starter...

IRVING: With Arnold Berkowitz.

ANNIE: When he makes the Detroit Red Wings, we're going to get married and move out of the Soo. *(Irving now turns and stares at Peter.)*

IRVING: Does Peter like you a lot?

ANNIE: I think so.

IRVING: I like you a lot too, you know...

ANNIE: Pete likes me in the romantic way...

IRVING: Oh, right... *(Annie and Irving walk from bedroom.)*

In this scene, Annie and Irving share advice and at least one good secret.

IRVING: You wouldn't know this on your own, but it's the tradition that every Bar Mitzvah boy makes a speech to the congregation which has to start with the words: "Today I am a Man," because on the day of a boy's Bar Mitzvah, he legally, in the Jewish laws, becomes a man. He becomes a full member of the congregation. He gets to sit downstairs with the men, because he's one of them. *(Suddenly.)* Are you *awake? (Irving leans over to Annie, who has been drifting into sleep.)* Annie!

ANNIE: I'm listening! I'm listening!

IRVING: I'm just getting to the best part.

ANNIE: I'm listening.

IRVING: *So.* There's Quentin...pockets stuffed with pens...standing up in front of five hundred people...sweating like a disgusting pig and he screams out with this dopey voice of his, "Todayyyy...I ammm...a *fountain pennn!*"

ANNIE: He didn't?

IRVING: He did! *(Annie and Irving roar with laughter.)*

ANNIE: It sounds like you and your father had a wonderful time together...

IRVING: Oh, yuh, we always do...It's more than wonderful. It's actually *two*derful.

ANNIE: *(Laughs.)* I think you're *ten*derful.

IRVING: Oh, yuh, well then you're *twent*derful...*(They both laugh again.)* What's Pete?

ANNIE: Oh, Pete's a *hundra*ful...

IRVING: *(Slightly depressed by this computation.)* Yuh, I guess... *(Pauses.)* How come your father doesn't like Pete?

ANNIE: 'Cause Pete's Italian. My father thinks the Italians keep the Ukrainians poor. The Italians control all the work at Algoma Steel and force the Ukrainians into terrible jobs...

IRVING: Is that true?

ANNIE: I don't think it's true...*(Pause.)* God, don't ever let on I said that! Can you keep a secret?

IRVING: Do I look like I can't?

ANNIE: I know you can. *(Whispers.)* I think my father's totally wrong. I think the Italians are fine people. I've met Pete's mother and father and his brother Robert, and his sister Carmella, and they're really all fine people.

IRVING: So, why don't you bring your father to meet them?

ANNIE: Oh, don't talk crazy! My father won't have anything to do with anything that's Italian, period.

IRVING: I thought you said he loves opera?

ANNIE: He loves opera more than he loves me or my mother or anything else in the whole world...on the planet Earth!

IRVING: But all the great operas are Italian!

ANNIE: No, they're not, silly! They're Canadian...

IRVING: They are not. They're Italian.

ANNIE: Irving, don't say that. My father would never listen to an opera if it were Italian...

IRVING: Annie, I should know, right. Music is my middle name...

ANNIE: Irving, are you trying to kid me? Because if you are, this isn't very funny!

IRVING: I swear to you: Verdi, Puccini...all of them: Italians...

ANNIE: The names *sound* Italian.

IRVING: Because they're Italian. I swear to you. I promise never to eat bacon when I grow up, if I'm lying. *(Pauses; whispers.)* I'm

planning to eat a great deal of bacon when I'm a man on my own
…which is something *my* parents made *me* promise not to do…
like your not seeing Peter, ever…

ANNIE: Oh, God, this is incredible news…

IRVING: I'm glad I was able to tell you…

ANNIE: Me, too. I really owe you a lot, Irving…*(Pauses.)* Irving?

IRVING: What?

ANNIE: You must never, ever in a million years let on that it was
me who let on, but your parents eat bacon all the time…

IRVING: Don't talk crazy! My mother would rather fall through
the ice…

ANNIE: It's in the Chinese food they eat at the Ritz Cafe with the
Rosens every Saturday night…

IRVING: That's what the brain-damaged, homo-putz Rosen said,
but he was just trying to get me in trouble…

ANNIE: It's true. It's the little red bits…

IRVING: No *wonder* I love the red bits! No *wonder!* God, Annie!
How could they just *lie* to me? How could they just look me
straight in the eye and lie to me? *How could they?*

ANNIE: They didn't exactly lie…It was more like, sort of breaking a
law than a lie…like driving a little too fast?

IRVING: But they knew it was bacon: they knew they were breaking
the Law. If you break the Law, you break the Law. You don't
break laws "a little"… That's a lot of crap!

ANNIE: Irving!

IRVING: Well, it is! How come they lied to me? How come?

ANNIE: I think we just have to accept the fact that sometimes parents
have impossible sets of rules.

IRVING: You mean like with bacon?

ANNIE: Well, yes…like with bacon. Or the way my parents are with
me…and Italians. They think that I should hate all Italians, just
because they do…

IRVING: Except for the Italians in opera.

ANNIE: *(Suddenly.)* Do you think I should stop seeing Pete? Do you
agree with my father?

IRVING: I think you should keep Pete Lisanti as your friend. That's
what *I* think.

ANNIE: Irving, if you promise not to tell I did it, I'm going to get you
a real meal of bacon. More bacon than you've ever seen…
(Pauses, then quickly.) I think that children should have their own

sets of rules…according to what *they* think is right and wrong, not their parents.

IRVING: What happens if parents find out about certain children having their own certain rules? Won't certain children get their behinds beaten black and blue?

ANNIE: Well, certain parents don't have to ever find out. It is possible for secrets to be kept secret, right?

IRVING: If you will cook me a bacon meal and never tell my parents, I will be your friend for life!

ANNIE: *(In Ukrainian.)* "Te brechaca mene."

IRVING: What does that mean?

ANNIE: That is "Kiss my behind" in Ukrainian.

IRVING: *That's* "Kiss my behind" in Ukrainian? "Te brechaca mene?" So, what's [Ukrainian words spoken at her arrival]… what I said to you on your first day?

ANNIE: You don't want to know.

IRVING: Oh, God, I do, I really do! *(Annie whispers horrifying obscenity into Irving's ear: a shared private moment. Shocked and thrilled.)* I said that??? *(He faints. Blackout.)*

TWELVE DREAMS
by James Lapine

The Characters: Jenny (18-20) and Emma (10)

This play was inspired by an actual case-history from the notebooks of the famous psychiatrist, Carl Jung. The characters and events of the play, however, are fictional. The story revolves around little Emma, whose father – a psychiatrist – is lost in grief over the death of his wife, Emma's mother; as a result, he neglects Emma. Poor Emma suffers a series of rather disturbing dreams, which she writes about in her journal. She shows the entries to her father, but he seems unable to understand them. Tragically, the twelve dreams foreshadow the death of the little girl.

In the scene below, Emma is talking to Jenny, her cousin by marriage. It is bedtime. Miss Banton is Emma's ballet teacher; Mrs. Trowbridge is a wealthy but neurotic patient of Emma's father.

(Emma's bedroom.)

JENNY: Emma, let's get into bed.

EMMA: I'm trying to find Orion's belt.

JENNY: *(Emphatically.)* Emma…

EMMA: Do you think anyone lives in space?

JENNY: No. I don't.

EMMA: But isn't that where heaven is?

JENNY: No one is sure where heaven is.

EMMA: But if it's not in space, where is it? *(No answer.)* I don't think Daddy believes there is a heaven.

JENNY: Why not?

EMMA: When I told him you said that was where Mommy was, he said you didn't have that information.

JENNY: *(Annoyed.)* Emma! Bed.

EMMA: Okay. *(Gets into bed.)* Jenny, I have an itch on my back. Would you scratch if for me?

JENNY: You seem to always have an itch around this time.

EMMA: Please…

JENNY: Okay. *(Jenny rubs Emma's back.)*

EMMA: Jenny, did my mother dress like Miss Banton or Mrs.

Trowbridge?

JENNY: *(Alarmed.)* How do you know Mrs. Trowbridge's name?

EMMA: *(Flippant.)* I just heard it one day.

JENNY: *(Grabbing her in anger.)* You have very big ears, young lady, and if you're not careful, somebody's going to snip them off!

EMMA: I'm sorry.

JENNY: *(Cools down and continues to rub Emma's back.)* No. Your mother did not dress like either of them. She was a very stylish woman though, Emma. Sometimes when we were growing up, I would get some of her "hand-me-downs." *(Joking.)* Unfortunately, they never looked quite the same on me.

EMMA: Am I going to look like her?

JENNY: Well, you have your mother's eyes, and I think our family's smile, but in many ways, you are your father's little girl.

EMMA: And what did Mother die from?

JENNY: *(Hesitant.)* She was very sick and she just died.

EMMA: Well, why do some people die and others don't?

JENNY: Emma, everyone dies. Some just die sooner than others.

EMMA: Did God make her die?

JENNY: *(Rubbing Emma's back.)* Emma, I think you should have this discussion with your father. Now stop with your endless questions.

EMMA: I'm sorry.

JENNY: *(Tucking her in.)* One thing is for sure. You have your father's mind.

EMMA: What kind of mind do you have, Jenny?

JENNY: At the moment, a very tired one. Now enough of this conversation. Say your prayers and I'll tuck you in. *(Music.)*

EMMA: Spread out thy wings, Lord Jesus mild,
And take to thee thy chick, thy child,
If Satan would devour it,
No harm shall overpower it,
So let the angels sing!

JENNY: Sleep tight, Emma. Sweet dreams. *(She kisses her.)*

EMMA: Good night, Jenny.

JENNY: Don't let the bed bugs bite!

(Emma giggles, as lights go to black.)

WHITE CHAMELEON
by Christopher Hampton

The Characters: Chris (10) and Paul (9-10)

It is September, 1956, and young Chris, an English boy, is living in Alexandria, Egypt, with his father and mother. His father is an engineer in the British military. The story is a memory of older Christopher's experiences living in Alexandria, told in flashback. Among the experiences, both pleasurable and troubling, is Chris's friendship with Ibrahim, the family's Egyptian house servant. Ibrahim not only serves the family, he has lots of opinions and a tendency to drink a bit too much. Chris has few friends.

In this scene, Albert and Fatima Etheridge, friends of Chris's parents, have come to visit, along with their timid son, Paul. Paul and Chris are left alone to play.

CHRIS: Is that a war wound your father has?

PAUL: No, motorcycle accident.

CHRIS: Do you know the French for "wound"?

PAUL: I don't do French.

CHRIS: It's *blessure*. I didn't know, so I put: 'The soldier's blessing is bleeding slowly.'
(This sinks like a stone as well: Chris rises to his feet, rattled.)
Shall we go and play?

PAUL: If you like.
(He gets up and follows Chris into the hall. But here Chris stops for a moment, looking up at the staircase.)

CHRIS: I can go up on the outside.

PAUL: What do you mean?

CHRIS: On the outside of the banister. I climb all the way up to the top.
(Paul looks up at the landing, frowning, seeing that the banister curves and continues along the landing to the far wall. He points up at it.)

PAUL: How do you get over that?

CHRIS: I can't. I just come down again and go up the proper way.

PAUL: I don't see the point of that.

CHRIS: It's just fun, that's all. I'll show you.

(He goes and stands sideways on the banister and climbs up a few steps on the outside. The margin is wide enough to make this perfectly safe, but not so wide that it's possible to ascend except sideways and moving one's feet carefully between the banisters, one step at a time.)

You want to try?

(Paul hesitates. He clearly doesn't, but, in the end, answers as brightly as he can.)

PAUL: Yes, all right.

(He begins cautiously to follow. He's agreeably surprised to find it much easier than he'd feared, but the strain is evident from his gritted teeth. Chris lets him catch up, then goes at a modest pace, so that he can keep up. About halfway up, after the first corner has been negotiated, he turns his head to Paul.)

CHRIS: All right?

PAUL: Yes, I'm fine.

(They carry on, all the way up to the top. There, Chris moves far enough along the landing, so that Paul has room to round the corner as well. They stand there for a moment, hanging on tight.)

CHRIS: There we are. It's good, isn't it?

(But there's no answer from Paul, whose eyes are screwed shut and whose head is bunched into his shoulders. Chris looks across at him with a trace of alarm.)

What's the matter, are you all right?

(Paul utters a kind of clenched sob.)

What's the matter, you just have to go down now.

PAUL: I can't.

CHRIS: Yes, you can, it's easier going down.

PAUL: I can't go first.

(He snuffles a bit, while Chris reviews the situation.)

CHRIS: All right, if you get as close as you can to the banisters, I can step round you and I'll go first.

PAUL: All right.

(He does his best to comply; but when Chris puts a hand on his shoulder blade, preparatory to his attempt to step around him, Paul seizes up.)

No.

CHRIS: What?

PAUL: It's no good, if you go past me, I won't be able to follow you down.

CHRIS: Why not?

PAUL: I can't move.

(Silence. Chris considers. Downstairs, Ibrahim dries his hands, exits through the screen door, blows his nose with practiced skill between thumb and forefinger and sets off towards his quarters at the foot of the garden.)

CHRIS: All right, if you let me by, I can go down and get someone to help.

PAUL: Who?

CHRIS: Ibrahim.

PAUL: Who?

CHRIS: Ibrahim.

PAUL: But that means you'll leave me alone.

CHRIS: Only for a minute. I'll come straight back.

PAUL: If you leave me on my own, I'll fall.

CHRIS: No, you won't.

PAUL: I will, I'll fall!

(Silence.)

CHRIS: I'm sure you'll be able to follow me down.

PAUL: No!

(There's an unmistakable note of hysteria in his voice now. Chris thinks a little more, and then calls out, tentatively.)

PAUL: Ibrahim.

(But Ibrahim is gone. Chris waits and then calls, louder.)
Ibrahim!
(No answer. Chris turns to Paul again.)
All right. You've got to help me, we've got to shout as loud as we can. Ready? Go. *(He starts yelling for Ibrahim at the top of his voice and, a moment later, Paul joins in. They shout for a while, to no avail. Then a deathly silence falls.)* Maybe they can hear us and they just think we're calling for Ibrahim. Maybe we'd better say something else.

PAUL: What?

CHRIS: Help.

(So they start again, there's no response and again, they fall silent.)
Won't you let me go and get someone?

PAUL: No, no, no!

(Silence again.)

MONOLOGUES
For
Girls

ALICE'S ADVENTURES IN WONDERLAND
Adapted by Craig Slaight
From the novel by Lewis Carroll

The Character: Alice (11)

Lewis Carroll's timeless classic creates a world of make-believe where anything can happen and often does. Little Alice tumbles into a most fantastic place and she meets some of the most unusual inhabitants one could ever imagine: the White Rabbit, the March Hare and Mad Hatter, the Caterpillar, Tweedledum and Tweedledee, the Queen of Hearts and, of course, Humpty Dumpty, to name a few. Alice has a remarkable visit and returns to her own world a little bit smarter than when she left.

Here are two of Alice's speeches that record that journey.

ALICE: (*Alice is falling down the rabbit hole.*) Well, after such a fall as this, I shall think nothing of tumbling down stairs. How brave they'll all think me at home! Why, I wouldn't say anything about it, even if I fell off the top of the house. (*She continues her fall, down and down.*) I wonder how many miles I've fallen by this time? I must be getting somewhere near the center of the earth. Let me see: that would be four thousand miles down, I think. Yes, that's about the right distance - but then I wonder what latitude or longitude I've got to? I wonder if I shall fall right *through* the earth! How funny it'll seem to come out among the people that walk with their heads downward! The Antipathies, I think, but I shall have to ask them what the name of the country is, you know. Please, Ma'am, is this New Zealand or Australia? (*She tries to courtesy.*) And what an ignorant little girl she'll think me for asking! No, it'll never do to ask: perhaps I shall see it written up somewhere. (*She continues falling down and down.*) Dinah'll miss me very much to-night, I should think. I hope they'll remember her saucer of milk at tea-time. Dinah, my dear! I wish you were down here with me! There are no mice in the air, I'm afraid, but you might catch a bat, and that's very like a mouse you know. But do cats eat bats, I wonder? (*She becomes*

sleepy.) Do bats eat cats? Do cats eat bats? Do bats eat cats? Do
cats eat bats? (*She is dozing off and beginning a dream about her
cat Dinah.*) Now Dinah, tell me the truth: did you ever eat a bat?

ALICE: Dear, dear! How queer everything is to-day! And yesterday
things went on just as usual. I wonder if I've been changed in the
night? Let me think: was I the same when I got up this morning?
I almost think I can remember feeling a little different. But if I'm
not the same, the next question is, who in the world am I? Ah,
that's the great puzzle! (*She thinks.*) I'm sure I'm not Ada for her
hair goes in such long ringlets, and mine doesn't go in ringlets at
all; and I'm sure I can't be Mabel, for I know all sorts of things,
and she, oh! she knows such a very little! Besides, *she's* she, and
I'm I, and - oh dear, how puzzling it all is! I'll try if I know all the
things I used to know. Let me see: four times five is twelve, and
four times six is thirteen, and four times seven is - oh dear! I shall
never get to twenty at that rate! However the multiplication table
doesn't signify: let's try geography. London is the capital of
Paris, and Paris is the capital of Rome, and Rome - no *that's* all
wrong, I'm certain! I must have been changed for Mabel! I'll try
to say 'How doth the little-'

> "*How doth the little crocodile
> Improve his shining tail,
> And pours the waters of the Nile
> On every golden scale!*
>
> *How cheerfully he seems to grin,
> How neatly spreads his claws,
> And welcomes little fishes in
> With gently smiling jaws!*"

I'm sure those are not the right words. I must be Mabel after all,
and I shall have to go and live in that poky little house, and have
next to no toys to play with, and oh! ever so many lessons to
learn! No I've made up my mind about it; if I'm Mabel, I'll stay
down here! It'll be no use their putting their heads down and
saying, 'Come up again, dear!' I shall only look up and say, 'Who

am I, then? Tell me that first, and then, if I like being that person, I'll come up; if not, I'll stay down here till I'm somebody else' - but, oh dear! (*She begins crying.*) I do wish they *would* put their heads down! I am so *very* tired of being all alone here!

AND THEY DANCE REAL SLOW IN JACKSON
by Jim Leonard, Jr.

The Character: Cindy Sue (10)

This play is the story of Elizabeth Ann Willow, a young girl confined
to a wheelchair because she was crippled at birth from cerebral palsy.
In the story we see how the prejudice and insensitive ignorance of the
people in Jackson (a fictitious small town in Indiana) destroy this
young woman. Throughout the play we hear from various people in
Elizabeth's life. In this scene from school we hear a class report from
Cindy Sue White.

CINDY SUE: "The Birth of Jackson, Indiana. By Cindy Sue White,
Room 5, Grade 5, Ernie Pyle School." *(Takes a breath.)* "Fort
Jackson was put up over one hundred years ago by General
Andrew Jackson while he was killing all the Indians in Indiana.
Him and his soldiers cut down trees and built it to sleep in. Then
the pioneers came and started farms. After that the walls fell down
and the pioneers decided to just call it Jackson instead of adding
the Fort part on since all the Indians was kilt anyhow. After that
them pioneers built a beer factory and started selling beer to
everyone else in Indiana. Jackson is famous for its good Pioneer
Beer...on account of they get the water for it from outa the river
and on account of the river having the coldest blackest water in
the world, practically..." *(She stops reading and throws her two
cents in.)* I asked my grampa how it got so cold and so black and
he says it's because the water flows from outa the dirt and mud
someplace up north – or something. It's so cold it ain't hardly
good for swimming in! If you ask me, what they oughta do is
dam the whole thing up and stick a heater in it...'cept then it'd
flood the graveyard and all of them bodies'd come floating up
outa the ground...old rotted pioneers and soldiers floating all over
Jackson! At least there ain't no Indians buried there...cause
Indian's ain't Christian, mostly...*(Back to paper.)* "The river is
famous in Jackson. When my grampa was born there were almost
five thousand people in Jackson and they had fifty different
churches – fifty of 'em! After that they built a four lane highway

with clover leafs and lines all over the place and everybody got on it and drove off to Evansville. Jackson is on the map of Indiana and on the United States of America map – but it ain't on no globes. We got close to three thousand people left and twelve churches counting the Catholics. They all go to the same one." *(Her personal conclusion.)* There ain't nothing here, really. 'Cept that dirty old river and a buncha fishes inside it. "By Cindy Sue White, Room 5, Grade 5, Ernie Pyle School."

APPROACHING ZANZIBAR
by Tina Howe

The Character: Pony (9)

The Blossom family are traveling by car across the country to visit Charlotte Blossom's dying aunt in Taos, New Mexico. Along the way, everyone in the family experiences something important, especially eighty-one year old Aunt Olivia. Here the young people help the old sort out their lives. In this speech, Pony confronts her fears about death with Aunt Olivia.

PONY: I get so scared thinking about it, I can't sleep. Every night I touch my bedside light 44 times and hold my breath for as long as I can and pray, *"Please, God, don't let me die! I'll be good, I'll be good!"* And then I start imagining what it will be like...You know, being dead in a coffin, being underground all alone in the dark.

[**OLIVIA:** What's that smell? I know, it's cloves...Cloves!]

PONY: ...with mice and, and spiders, and worms crawling over me... and, and dead people moaning all around me...and trying to call Mommy and Daddy but they can't hear me because I'm so far under ground... *(Olivia breaths heavily. Pony getting more and more upset.)* And, then I start thinking about being there forever and ever and ever and ever until my body's a skeleton...a clattery skeleton with grinning teeth and no eyes, and I touch my night light 144 times so it will go away, and then 244 times, and 444 times, and I get crying so hard Mommy has to come in and hold me...And, and...Oh no, it's starting to happen now...Could I get in bed with you? *(Climbs in next to her, whimpering.)* I don't want to die, I don't want to die...

DAISY FAY AND THE MIRACLE MAN
by Fannie Flagg

The Character: Daisy (11)

Fannie Flagg's comic and heart-felt novel concerns the life journey of
Daisy Fay, a young girl growing up in the Gulf Coast area of Florida.
The book covers seven years of Daisy's life, told as diary entries. In
the private glimpse that Daisy's frank record gives us, we have a
picture of an exciting childhood. Daisy's unique personality and
adventurous spirit provide an intriguing character study, filled with
laughs and thoughts for contemplation.

   Here are four entries from Daisy's diary.

April 2, 1952

   Momma had her heart set on me playing the harp after someone once
said I looked like a little angel. There wasn't anybody in Jackson who
would teach harp music, so she settled on tap dancing. The Neva Jean
School of Tap and Ballet promised to have your child on their toes in
thirty days. The school was on top of the Whatley Drugstore, where
they make the best banana splits in the whole world. I was a petal in
the recital called "Springtime in Greentime" with a special number by
the Gainer Triplets, who played a three-leaf clover. Skooter Olgerson
was cast as a weed, but his momma didn't want him playing a weed
and she yanked him out of the show. I didn't do too good in the recital.
I was not in step but once.

   Momma let me quit when I ruined all her hardwood floors practicing
my shuffleball chain. Besides, Neva Jean said I was holding the whole
class back. The only fun I ever had in that dance class was the day
when Buster Sessions showed up in tap shoes that were too big for
him. He is a real sissy and when his momma came to see him in the
class, he got to tapping so fast, showing off, that one of his shoes flew
off and hit the piano player, Mrs. Vella Fussel, in the back. Buster's
mother wasn't even looking. She was sitting there in a fold-up chair,
chewing a whole pack of Juicy Fruit gum and reading *Screen Secrets.*

April 12, 1952

Dr. Clyde told Momma that my tonsils would have to come out and that it would be a snap. He talked all about the ice cream I could eat and what fun it would be, and Momma took me to the Rexall and bought me a Sparkle Plenty doll.

When I got to the hospital, Dr. Clyde promised me my momma and daddy would be with me the whole time. Then they put me on this table and rolled me down the hall. I was OK until we got to these two big screen doors and my momma and daddy were told they would have to wait outside. I sat right up when I heard that. Momma and Daddy were looking scared, but those people in the hospital rolled me in the room alone and closed the doors.

Then some other people with masks started fooling around and even tried to take my Sparkle Plenty doll away. They asked if I was Catholic, and then they put this strainer on my face and tried to kill me with ether, one of the worst-smelling things I have ever smelled in my life.

When I heard a commotion outside the door, I tried to get up, but five against a little child is not fair. It was the worst experience of my life. I heard bells, sirens and saw terrible things. I dreamed a story about a magician with a magic stick that scared me to death.

I found out later that as I was being rolled into the operating room Momma turned to say something to Daddy, but Daddy had run down to the end of the hall and shut himself into a telephone booth. Some doctors got him out and gave him a shot, he was so upset. I love him, but Daddy isn't much help in a real-life crisis.

Don't ever let them fool you with that ice cream stuff. I couldn't even taste it and didn't want it, to boot. After I got my strength back, I opened up the head of my Sparkle Plenty doll and pulled the eyes out.

Grandma Pettibone came over to the hospital and fanned me with a bingo card and I got to miss school, but, other than that, the hospital was a pain.

August 8, 1952

I found out I got ringworm from Felix. If it gets in my head, they will have to shave off my hair. I'll be bald just like Eisenhower, and I am a Democrat.

The doctor said it's one of the worst cases he's ever seen. Momma has to put purple medicine, called itch-me-not, all over me. I have purple circles everywhere.

That woman who is crazy over accessories finally came to the Jr. Debutantes' Club. You wouldn't believe it. Everybody was getting excited over a bunch of scarves and gloves and pearl collars. She said with the right accessories you can dress up any outfit. She had on a black dress and she kept adding pop beads and all kinds of things.

She thought it changed the way she looked, but it didn't. She said the well-dressed woman had a complete wardrobe of accessories for every occasion. At the end of her talk she set up shop and tried to sell us things.

I might have bought something from her, but Kay Bob Benson screamed, "She's got ringworm," and they wouldn't let me try anything on. That woman stayed away from me because I had white stuff on my face and purple rings all over me. I would liked to have had some pop beads, but you can't buy anything unless you try it on.

Kay Bob Benson won't get anywhere near me because she is afraid of getting ringworm in her hair and she is crazy about her hair. Her mother takes her to Magnolia Springs to Nita's Beauty Box every week and gets her hair fixed like Jane Powell's. She looks as much like Jane Powell as I look like the Queen of Sheba. I'm not invited to her stupid birthday party because of the ringworm, so just as I was leaving Jr. Debutantes, I went over when she wasn't looking and said, "Happy birthday," and gave her a big birthday kiss right on the face. She about squealed her head off and ran in the live bait store to the sink and scrubbed her whole head and ruined her Jane Powell hairdo.

Momma is going to make me send her a birthday present. I am going to find out what perfume has the most bobcat pee in it. Or maybe I could give her a jar of Daddy's hemorrhoid medicine with the rubber finger in it.

Mrs. Dot's thought for the day was: "Fashionable people never wear evening clothes in the daytime unless, of course, they are being buried."

August 13, 1952

Jessie LeGore, the fat boy on Cotton Bayou, died. He sent me a sweetheart pillow because I had made him laugh once. I wish I had gone back to see him. I could have told him some jokes or done my Mario Lanza impersonation. He never hurt anyone. I don't think anyone should have to die.

Sometimes, in the middle of the night, I wake up and remember that I am going to have to die and it scares me so bad that I break out in a cold sweat and I go get in the bed with Momma and Daddy. Maybe by the time I grow up they will find a cure for dying and I won't have to worry.

If anything happened to my mommy and daddy, I couldn't stand it. I saw *Bambi* when I was five and when Bambi's mother got burned to death after she said, "Run, Bambi, run," I started screaming and crying so loud they had to take me out of the theater. I wouldn't let go of my mother for days. I can't think about that fire without getting sick to my stomach. If I do die, I hope it is the end of the world, so I won't be alone.

Connie said they couldn't get Jessie out of his room. He was so fat they had to tear the house apart, and it took fifteen men to pull him to his grave.

This sweetheart pillow is the first gift I ever got from a dead person. He must have known he was going to die, but he couldn't get up and run. I would run so fast that nothing could catch me. I believe you can outrun death. I don't even want to think what my momma and daddy would do if I died. Momma said I am the only reason she is living and if she didn't have me, she would take a gun and blow her brains out. She stays with Daddy just so I will have a father. If it wasn't for me, she would have left him a long time ago.

Daddy said he wouldn't want to live if anything happened to me. I take very good care of myself for that reason.

When I told Michael that Jessie had died, all he wanted to know was how much did he weigh and how big was the grave. I don't think Michael ever saw *Bambi*.

FAREWELL TO MANZANAR
by Jeanne Wakatsuki Houston and James D. Houston

The Character: Jeanne Wakatsuki (11-13)

Jeanne Wakatsuki was among the 10,000 Japanese Americans who were interned in a camp called Manzanar (which means apple orchard) during World War II. Taken from their home in Long Beach, California, having no time to settle their belongings, the family struggled to keep together and conserve their traditions in a hostile and disturbing environment.

Here are three different glimpses of life for a young girl growing up at Manzanar.

As the months at Manzanar turned to years, it became a world unto itself, with its own logic and familiar ways. In time, staying there seemed far simpler than moving once again to another, unknown place. It was as if the war were forgotten, our reason for being there forgotten. The present, the little bit of busywork you had right in front of you, became the most urgent thing. In such a narrowed world, in order to survive, you learn to contain your rage and your despair, and you try to re-create, as well as you can, your normality, some sense of things continuing. The fact that America has accused us, or excluded us, or imprisoned us, or whatever it might be called, did not change the kind of world we wanted. Most of us were born in this country; we had no other models. Those parks and gardens lent it an oriental character, but in most ways it was a totally equipped American small town, complete with schools, churches, Boy Scouts, beauty parlors, neighborhood gossip, fire and police departments, glee clubs, softball leagues, Abbott and Costello movies, tennis courts, and traveling shows. (I still remember an Indian who turned up one Saturday billing himself as a Sioux chief, wearing bear claws and head feathers. In the firebreak he sang songs and danced his tribal dances while hundreds of us watched.

In our family, while Papa puttered Mama made her daily rounds to the mess halls, helping young mothers with their feeding, planning diets for the various ailments people suffered from. She wore a bright yellow, longbilled sun hat she had made herself and always kept stiffly starched. Afternoons I would see her coming from blocks away, heading home, her tiny figure warped by heat waves and that bonnet a yellow flower wavering in the glare.

Outside of school we had a recreation program, with leaders hired by the War Relocation Authority. During the week they organized games and craft activities. On weekends we often took hikes beyond the fence. A series of picnic groups and camping sites had been built by internees – clearings, with tables, benches and toilets. The first was about half a mile out, the farthest several miles into the Sierras. As restrictions gradually loosened, you could measure your liberty by how far they'd let you go – to Camp Three with a Caucasian, to Camp Four alone. As fourth- and fifth-graders we usually hiked out to Camp One, on the edge of Bair's Creek, where we could wade, collect rocks and sit on the bank eating lunches the mess hall crew packed for us. I would always take along a quart jar and a white handkerchief and sit for an hour next to the stream, watching it strain through the cloth, trickling under the glass. Water there was the clearest I've ever seen, running right down off the snow.

One of our leaders on those excursions was a pretty young woman named Lois, about twenty-five at the time, who wore long braids, full skirts, and peasant blouses. She was a Quaker, like so many of the Caucasians who came in to teach and do volunteer work. She also had a crush on a tall, very handsome and popular Nisei boy who sometimes sang and danced in talent shows. His name was Isao. In order to find a little free time together, Lois and Isao arranged an overnight camping trip for all the girls in our class. We took jars for water, potatoes to roast, and army blankets and hiked up Bair's Creek one Friday afternoon to a nice little knoll at the base of the mountains.

All the girls were tittering and giggling at the way Isao and Lois held hands and looked at each other. They built us a big driftwood fire that night, and told us ghost stories until they figured we had all dozed off. Then they disappeared for a while into the sagebrush. I was still awake and heard their careful footsteps and snapping twigs. I thought how hard it would be to walk around out there without a flashlight. It was years later that I remembered and understood what that outing must have meant for them. At the time I had my own escape to keep me occupied. In truth, I barely noticed their departure. This was the first overnight camping trip I'd ever made. For me it was enough to be outside the barracks for a night, outside the square mile of wire, next to a crackling blaze and looking at stars so thick and so close to the ground I could have reached up and scooped out an armful.

Most of the Japanese returning to the coast resettled without suffering bodily harm. But gossip tends to thrive on bad news, not good. Stories such as these spread through the camp and grew in our minds like tumors. I remember hearing them discussed in our barracks, quietly, as if Ku Klux Klansmen lurked outside the window, the same way my brothers discussed our dilemma during the brief stay in Boyle Heights, before the evacuation.

I would listen to the stories and I would cringe. And this was both odd and confusing to me, because ever since we'd arrived, the outside world had loomed in my imagination as someplace inaccessible yet wonderfully desirable. I would recall our days in Ocean Park. I would flip through the Sears, Roebuck catalogue, dreaming of the dresses and boots and coats that were out there somewhere at the other end of the highway beyond the gate. All the truly good things, it often seemed, the things we couldn't get, were outside, and had to be sent for, or shipped in. In this sense, God and the Sears, Roebuck catalogue were pretty much one and the same thing in my young mind.

Once, during a novena at the Maryknoll chapel, I had asked for something I desperately longed for and had never seen inside the camp. We were told to ask for something we really wanted. We were to write it on a piece of paper, pray devoutly for nine days, and if we'd prayed well it would be answered. The nuns expected us to ask for purity of soul, or a holy life. I asked God for some dried apricots. I wrote this on a piece of paper, dropped it into the prayer box, and began to fantasize about how they would arrive, in a package from Sears, Roebuck. I knew how they would taste, and feel in my hands. I said my rosary, thirty times a day, for nine days, and for nine more days after that I waited. The dried apricots never came. My faith in God and in the Catholic church slipped several notches that time. But not my faith in *the outside,* where all such good things could be found. I went back to flipping through the catalogue.

LITTLE WOMEN
Adapted by Roger Wheeler
From the Novel by Louisa May Alcott

The Character: Amy (12)

Set in Concord, Massachusetts, during the Civil War era, this dramatization of Alcott's popular, uplifting, and very human tale about Jo, Meg, Beth and Amy includes the most memorable scenes from the book. From Jo's writing the Christmas Play and the sisters spending their Christmas money for presents for their mother, through the touching scenes with Beth when the Angel of Death seems near, to the end when the girls are married – Wheeler's adaptation captures the spirit and hope of humankind everywhere.

In the first speech below, the sisters have been writing letters to their Mother. Here Amy reads her letter.

AMY: *(Reading.)* "Ma Chère Mama! We are all very well and I do my lessons always and never corroborate the girls – Meg says I mean 'contradick' so I put in both words and you can take the properest. Meg is a great comfort to me and lets me have jelly every night at tea it's so good for me Jo says because it keeps me sweet-tempered. Laurie is not respeckful as he ought to be now I am in my teens. He calls me 'Chick' and hurts my feelings. The sleeves of my blue dress were all worn out, and Meg put in new ones, but the full front came wrong and they are more blue than the dress. I felt bad but did not fret. I bear my troubles well but I do wish Hannah would put more starch in my aprons and have buckwheats every day. Can't she?"
(Turns to Meg and shows her letter.)
Didn't I make that interrigation point nice, Meg?
(Continues to read letter.)
"Meg says my punchtuation and spelling are disgraceful and I am mortyfied but dear me I have so many things to do I can't stop. Adieu! I send heaps of love to Papa. Your affectionate daughter, Amy Curtis March."

In the second speech, Amy reads her Last Will and Testament. Her sister Beth has been suffering from the fever, and because Amy feels that life is uncertain, she wants her wishes known.

AMY: *(Stands and reads importantly.)* "MY LAST WILL AND TESTAMENT! I, Amy Curtis March, being in my sane mind, do give and bequeathe all my earthly property viz. to wit: – namely. To my father, my best pictures, sketches, maps and works of art, including frames. To my mother, all my clothes, except the blue apron with the pockets, also my medal, with much love. To my dear sister Margaret, I give my turkquoise ring –" *(Aside to Laurie.)* If Aunt March gives it to me. *(Reads.)* "To Jo I leave my breast-pin, the one mended with sealing wax, also my bronze inkstand, and my most precious plaster rabbit, because I'm sorry I burnt up her story book. To Beth –" *(Aside to Laurie.)* If she lives after me. *(Reads.)* "To Beth I give my dolls and the little bureau, and my new slippers if she can wear them being thin when she gets well. To my friend and neighbor, Theodore Lawrence, I bequeathe my clay model of a horse though he did say it hasn't any neck. To our venerable benefactor, Mr. Lawrence, I leave my purple box. And now having disposed of my most valuable property I hope all will be satisfied and not blame the dead. I forgive everyone, and trust we shall all meet when the trump shall sound. Amen! To This Will and Testiment I set my hand and seal. Anni Domino, 1862. Amy Curtis March. Witnessed by –" *(Turns to Laurie and shows him the paper.)* See! This is where you sign it, Laurie – on this line. Will you?

PETER PAN
by James Barrie

The Character: Peter (12)

This enchanting tale of the lost boys and their leader, Peter Pan, the little boy who doesn't want to grow up, has entertained readers and audiences for generations. Barrie's stage adaptation of his own book contains all of the memorable characters and episodes: Tinker Bell, the Darling family, Captain Hook and all of his pirates, and of course old Crock.

In the two speeches below, Peter talks to Tinker Bell.

*Editor's Note: Although this role is traditionally played by a female, the editors feel that it is outstanding material for both boys and girls to explore.

PETER: *(Stirring.)* Who is that?
> *(Tink has to tell her tale, in one long ungrammatical sentence.)*
> Wendy and the boys captured by the pirates! I'll rescue her, I'll rescue her!
> *(He leaps first at his dagger, and then at his grindstone, to sharpen it. Tink alights near the shell, and rings out a warning cry.)*
> Oh, that is just my medicine. Poisoned? Who could have poisoned it? I promised Wendy to take it, and I will as soon as I have sharpened my dagger.
> *(Tink, who sees its red colour and remembers the red in the Pirate's eye, nobly swallows the draught as Peter's hand is reaching for it.)*
> Why, Tink, you have drunk my medicine!
> *(She flutters strangely about the room, answering him now in a very thin tinkle.)*
> It was poisoned and you drank it to save my life! Tink, dear Tink, are you dying?
> *(He has never called her dear Tink before, and for a moment she is gay; she alights on his shoulder, gives his chin a loving bite, whispers "You silly ass," and falls on her tiny bed. The boudoir,*

*which is lit by her, flickers ominously. He is on his knees by the
opening.)*
Her light is growing faint, and if it goes out, that means she is
dead! Her voice is so low I can scarcely tell what she is saying.
She says – she says she thinks she could get well again if children
believed in fairies!
*(He rises and throws out his arms – he knows not to whom,
perhaps to the boys and girls of whom he is not one.)*
Do you believe in fairies? Say quick that you believe! If you
believe, clap your hands!
*(Many clap, some don't, a few hiss. Then perhaps there is a rush
of Nanas to the nurseries to see what on earth is happening. But
Tink is saved.)*
Oh, thank you, thank you, thank you! And now to rescue Wendy!

PETER: Tink, where are you? Quick, close the window. *(It closes.)*
Bar it. *(The bar slams down.)* Now when Wendy comes she will
think her mother has barred her out, and she will have to come
back to me!
(Tinker Bell sulks.)
Now, Tink, you and I must go out by the door.
*(Doors, however, are confusing things to those who are used to
windows, and he is puzzled when he finds that this one does not
open on to the firmament. He tries another, and sees the piano
player.)*
It is Wendy's mother!
(Tink pops on to his shoulder and they peep together.)
She is a pretty lady, but not so pretty as my mother. *(This is a pure
guess.)* She is making the box say "Come home, Wendy." You
will never see Wendy again, lady, for the window is barred!
*(He flutters about the room joyously like a bird, but has to return
to that door.)*
She has laid her head down on the box. There are two wet things
sitting on her eyes. As soon as they go away another two come
and sit on her eyes.
(She is heard moaning, "Wendy, Wendy, Wendy.")
She wants me to unbar the window. I won't! She is awfully fond
of Wendy. I am fond of her too. We can't both have her, lady! *(A
funny feeling comes over him.)* Come on, Tink; we don't want any
silly mothers.

PICTURE ME
by Margery Kreitman

The Character: Audrey (8)

Picture Me is the story of Audrey, an adult painter who attempts to reconcile the troubles in her adult life by recounting the experiences of her youth, particularly the almost mother-daughter relationship she had with Rosie, the family's black domestic. Throughout the play we see Audrey as an adult and at various stages in her youth.

Here, eight-year-old Audrey recounts a dream to Rosie, who has been with her since birth and is the dearest person to her heart. Rosie has just been told by Audrey's mother, Cele, that she is no longer needed in her position and must leave.

AUDREY: *(Singing, off stage.)* "RING AROUND THE ROSIE, POCKET FULL OF –" ROSIE?...ROSIE, ARE YOU STILL HERE? *(Child in pajamas runs in, panicked)* Ros-ie! You're still here! Oh, I'm so glad! *(Climbs up on Rosie's lap.)* Rosie, I had a bad dream. 'Member when we went to the amusement park that time and we were looking in those funny mirrors? Well, I dreamed we were there again. In the beginning, we were laughing and being silly, seeing ourselves real fat and short and then, real, real skinny and tall. But then...we went to this next mirror. First, I looked. It was the same me as always. No different. I didn't get it. I thought maybe it was a joke like the one that's inside the empty cage at the zoo. "THE MOST DANGEROUS ANIMAL ON EARTH," it says over it. And when you look into the mirror, you see yourself. But this one, this one didn't have a sign or anything. And it wasn't a cage. Anyway, it was your turn. You went up to the same mirror and you stood right in front, just like I did. Only this time it was different, 'cause...'cause nobody was looking back! The mirror was blank. It was really strange. You thought it was some kind of trick. So the next time we both stood in front of it together. And the same thing happened! I was there in the mirror, but you weren't. So, then, you went right up close to it, to see if you could see what the trick was, and then the strangest, most strangest thing happened of all. You disappeared! Right into the mirror! Just like in Alice in Wonderland! But it wasn't funny this time. It was scary. I hated it. I just wanted to wake up. I screamed, really, really, really loud. "HELP! HELP!" But nobody heard me. Then I screamed again, "HELP! HELP! SOMEBODY COME!" But nobody came. *(A beat.)* And then I woke up.

REINDEER SOUP
by Joe Pintauro

The Character: Julie (12)

Julie's mother died two years ago in a car accident. When her father
loses his job at an automobile factory in Detroit, he takes the children
to the northernmost region of Canada. Pop hopes to find a better life
for his family and a new job. When winter comes, and Pop still doesn't
have a job, the money runs out and food is scarce. The family is barely
surviving on a large pot of soup, made from occasional animals Pop
kills on the road. Julie is a devoted vegetarian, refusing to eat any
meat. She is so hungry she often loses grip on reality. Furious that her
father has caused this current situation, and still refusing his constant
urging to eat the soup, Julie argues for her belief.

JULIE: *(Hands over her ears.)* I wasn't meant for this world. I'm
wasting away, worrying about the elephants getting shot by
poachers so some narcissistic bimbo could wear an ivory bracelet.
I go to sleep each night wondering: how does that poor elephant
feel? She's got her trunk up in the trees grabbing fruit for her baby
and BAMMMM! Mother is hit. Mother is dizzy. Run, my darling
child. Mother is falling to her knees. Oh the pain. I'm bleeding to
death. Goodbye tree, goodbye clouds, BOOOOOM! I've fallen in
a heap. My eyes are glaring – my trunk is swinging wildly. Oh no.
They're coming closer. They're going to shoot again. The gun is
touching my skull. BAMMMMM! In the brain. Goodbye light!
The last thing I see is the giraffes running. The eagles soar up and
away. They look down and see the cities covered in pollution...
where will we go? The condors too. They swear to the god of all
flying creatures they will never lay their eggs again. And how
many people eat chickens each day? Twenty million? A hundred
million? All those chickens murdered each day. All that blood all
over the world. I think I'm going to faint. And now you tell me
that stringbeans and broccoli feel it too. I just won't stand for it
another minute. I'd rather...I'd rather...

YOU'RE A GOOD MAN, CHARLIE BROWN

*From the play script of a musical entertainment based on the
comic strip,* Peanuts *by Charles M. Schultz
Music, lyrics, and adaptation by Clark Gesner*

The Character: Lucy

Charles M. Schultz created a lovable set of characters that entertained
the world in newspapers for years and year. Clark Gesner's truthful
musical adaptation brought the characters to life on the stage and
appealed to young and old alike. There is an ageless quality to these
children (and one imaginative and frisky dog named Snoopy). The
struggles of one Charlie Brown to be recognized in this life, the
complications of friendships and relationships, the search for happiness
and personal integrity, infuse this story. These are struggles that apply
to people of all ages. Here, Mr. Schultz (with the help of Mr. Gesner)
has given us all a genuine opportunity to laugh, and feel, and to maybe
learn something. Lucy, a dynamic young lady with opinions that are
bold and unchangeable, tells Linus of her dream of becoming a Queen.

SPECIAL NOTE: The editors have included Linus' lines for the actor
to understand the responses. This piece could be used as a scene as
well, but as presented here, it works very well as a monologue.

LUCY: Linus, do you know what I intend? I intend to be a queen.
   When I grow up I'm going to be the biggest queen there ever was,
   and I'll live in this big palace with a big front lawn, and have lots
   of beautiful dresses to wear. And when I go out in my coach, all
   the people...
[**LINUS:** Lucy.]
LUCY:...all the people will wave and I will shout at them, and...
[**LINUS:** Lucy, I believe "queen" is an inherited title. (*Lucy is silent*)
   Yes, I'm quite sure. A person can only become a queen by being
   born into a royal family of the correct lineage so that she can
   assume the throne after the death of the reigning monarch. I can't
   think of any possible way that you could ever become a queen.
   (*Lucy is still silent*) I'm sorry, Lucy, but it's true.]

LUCY: (*Silence, and then*) ... and in the summertime I will go to my summer palace and I'll wear my crown in swimming and everything, and all the people will cheer and I will shout at them... (*Her vision pops*) What do you mean I can't be a queen.

[**LINUS:** It's true.]

LUCY: There must be a loophole. This kind of thing always has a loophole. Nobody should be kept from being a queen if she wants to be one. IT'S UNDEMOCRATIC!

[**LINUS:** Good grief.]

LUCY: It's usually just matter of knowing the right people. I'll bet a few pieces of well-placed correspondence and I get to be a queen in no time.

[**LINUS:** I think I'll watch television. (*He returns to the set*)]

LUCY: I know what I'll do. If I can't be a queen, then I'll be very rich. I'll work and work until I'm very very rich, and then I will buy myself a queendom.

[**LINUS:** Good grief.]

LUCY: Yes, I will buy myself a queendom and then I'll kick out the old queen and take over the whole operation myself. I will be head queen. And when I go out in my coach, all the people will wave, and I will...I will...

(*She has glanced at the TV set and become engrossed.*)

MONOLOGUES
For
Boys

BIG RIVER: The Adventures of Huckleberry Finn
(A Musical Play)
Book by William Hauptman Lyrics by Roger Miller
Adapted from the novel by Mark Twain

The Character: Huck (13-14)

This popular Broadway musical is a faithful and rousing retelling of Mark Twain's great American classic, *The Adventures of Huckleberry Finn*. Set along the Mississippi River Valley in the 1840s, Young Huck escapes his Pap and The Widow Douglas and all of the other restrictions of civilization with his companion Jim, a runaway slave. They set off down the great Mississippi on a raft, and along the way encounter some of the most colorful characters in American literature, including those oily conmen the Duke and the King. After a considerable journey, Huck decides to head out to the western territories before Tom Sawyer's Aunt Sally has a chance to adopt him and tame him once and for all.

Here Huck tells of his escape and his dream to be nothing but himself.

HUCK: The sky looks ever so deep when you look up in the moonlight. Everything was dead quiet, and it looked late, and *smelt* late – you know what I mean. Just me and the drift logs and the moon.
(He drags the canoe ashore on Jackson's Island.)
When I got to Jackson's Island, I was tired and sort of lonesome. There ain't no better way to put in time when you are lonesome than sleep. You can't stay so; you soon get over it. So I slept for the better part of three days.
(When the sun rises, Huck lies in a cool green glade, filled with the sound of singing birds.)
I was woke up by this deep boom.
(Thump of a cannon going off. Huck looks through his spyglass. Through a scrim upstage, we see the people board the ferry.)
Through my spyglass I seen the ferryboat crossing the river. They were firing off a cannon to make my body rise to the top – 'cause

that's supposed to go right to a drowned carcass and stop. Then I knowed my plan had worked and they thought I was dead. There's Pap...and Judge Thatcher...and the widow and Miss Watson...and Ben Rogers and Jo Harper, and there's Tom Sawyer! *(Laughs.)* The look on their faces!

[**WIDOW DOUGLAS:** Huckleberry! Huckleberry!]

(The ferryboat is gone.)

HUCK: But when they were gone, I felt almost lonely again. So I started exploring the island. I was the boss of it; it all belonged to me, so to say. And I was thinking: here was a place where a body didn't have to be nobody but himself.

A CHRISTMAS MEMORY
by Truman Capote

The Character: Buddy (7)

Truman Capote's touching short story recalls the friendship of two
distant cousins who lived in the same house for a few years of their
lives: one, a seven-year-old boy; the other, a gentle but spritely woman
in her sixties. Buddy's older cousin is still living in her childhood;
cared for, but barely tolerated, by the other adults in the house. While
her temperament and antics disturb the adults, Buddy adores her and
the time they spend together. The two share a special bond – a
friendship that surpasses age. The story recounts a series of Christmas
activities, from the making and gift-giving of fruitcakes, to building
and flying a wonderful kite on Christmas Day. It is also the story of the
quality of friendship. Buddy's special cousin is the cornerstone of his
memory – a memory that has lasted throughout his life.

In this speech, Buddy recalls the careful preparations for the making
of the fruitcakes.

It's always the same: a morning arrives in November, and my
friend, as though officially inaugurating the Christmas time of year that
exhilarates her imagination and fuels the blaze of her heart, announces:
"It's fruitcake weather! Fetch our buggy. Help me find my hat."

The hat is found, a straw cartwheel corsaged with velvet roses out-
of-doors has faded: it once belonged to a more fashionable relative.
Together, we guide our buggy, a dilapidated baby carriage, out to the
garden and into a grove of pecan trees. The buggy is mine; that is, it
was bought for me when I was born. It is made of wicker, rather
unraveled, and the wheels wobble like a drunkard's legs. But it is a
faithful object; springtimes, we take it to the woods and fill it with
flowers, herbs, wild fern for our porch pots; in the summer, we pile it
with picnic paraphernalia and sugar-cane fishing poles and roll it down
to the edge of a creek; it has its winter uses, too: as a truck for hauling
firewood from the yard to the kitchen, as a warm bed for Queenie, our
tough little orange and white terrier who has survived distemper and
two rattle-snake bites. Queenie is trotting beside it now.

Three hours later we are back in the kitchen hulling a heaping buggyload of windfall pecans. Our backs hurt from gathering them: how hard they were to find [the main crop having been shaken off the trees and sold by the orchard's owners, who are not us] among the concealing leaves, the frosted, deceiving grass. Caarackle! A cheery crunch, scraps of miniature thunder sound as the shells collapse and the golden mound of sweet oily ivory meat mounts in the milk-glass bowl. Queenie begs to taste, and now and again my friend sneaks her a mite, though insisting we deprive ourselves. "We mustn't, Buddy. If we start, we won't stop. And there's scarcely enough as there is. For thirty cakes." The kitchen is growing dark. Dusk turns the window into a mirror: our reflections mingle with the rising moon as we work by the fireside in the firelight. At last, when the moon is quite high, we toss the final hull into the fire and, with joined sighs, watch it catch flame. The buggy is empty, the bowl is brimful.

CONVICTS

by Horton Foote

The Character: Horace (13)

Horace Robedaux is all alone. He doesn't have a place with his family. His father divorced his mother and has died, leaving no money and no home. Horace's mother and sister, Lily Dale, have moved to Houston to find a home and work, but there wasn't room for Horace. Horace is left to stay at a decrepit plantation, worked by the convicts from the neighboring prison. All that is really important to Horace right now is to make enough money to put a tombstone on his father's grave.

Horace has been left to watch over a chained convict who has attempted to run away.

HORACE: I came out here from Harrison in June when the hands that work the plantations around here had money to buy groceries from the store. I came out to help out my uncle, but I ended up doing all the work because he spent all his time up at Mr. Soll's house gambling. I hope to earn enough money out here to put a tombstone on my daddy's grave.
(Pause. In the distance a convict sings "Ain't No More Cane On the Brazos.")
HORACE: I was out this way once before – during a storm, a terrible one. I ran away from home when the storm was just starting, and I got lost and ended upon the Brodler brothers' plantation, a little way up the river from here. They got drunk during the storm and stayed on a drunk for a month afterwards. They were two old bachelor brothers: Clarence and Murray Brodler. They're both dead now. About two months ago, after I left there, they were in Harrison drinking in Dawdy's Saloon, and they got into an argument with Jessie Shatther, and he got his gun and killed Murray and wounded Clarence, but Clarence got away before he could kill him too. He left there and went back to some place in Tennessee where he came from, and he let his hair grow long and he grew a beard and he came back here and no one recognized him, and he went into Dawdy's Saloon and got a friend

to watch out for Jessie Shatther, and when he walked into the saloon, he pulled out a pistol and killed him. A month later he got into a fight with William Jenkins and he got killed. The Brodler brothers were terrors. *(Pause.)* My name is Horace. *(Pause.)* What's your name?

A DEATH IN THE FAMILY
by James Agee

The Character: Rufus (6-7)

James Agee's touching novel won the Pulitzer Prize. It is the story of a family who lose their father in a tragic accident and then must survive without him. The focus of the story is on young Rufus as he perceives the world from a child's point of view.

In this speech, Rufus contemplates his life in the waking-darkness of the night.

Gentle, gentle dark.
My darkness. Do you listen? Oh, are you hollowed, all one taking ear?
My darkness. Do you watch me? Oh, are you rounded, all one guardian eye?
Oh, gentlest dark. Gentlest, gentlest night. My darkness. My dear darkness.

Under your shelter all things come and go.
Children are violent and valiant, they run and they shout like the winners of impossible victories, but before long now, even like me, they will be brought into their sleep.
Those who are grown great talk with confidence and are at all times skillful to serve and to protect, but before long now they too, before long, even like me, will be taken in and put to bed.
Soon come those hours when no one wakes. Even the locusts, even the crickets, silent shall be, as frozen brooks
In your great sheltering.

I hear my father; I need never fear.
I hear my mother; I shall never be lonely, or want for love.
When I am hungry it is they who provide for me; when I am in dismay, it is they who fill me with comfort.
When I am astonished or bewildered, it is they who make the weak ground firm beneath my soul: it is in them that I put my trust.
When I am sick it is they who send for the doctor; when I am well

and happy, it is in their eyes that I know best that I am loved; and it is towards the shining of their smiles that I lift up my heart and in their laughter that I know my best delight.

I hear my father and my mother and they are my giants, my king and my queen, beside whom there are no other so wise or worthy or honorable or brave or beautiful in this world.

I need never fear: nor ever shall I lack for loving-kindness.

THE HAPPY PRINCE
by Oscar Wilde

The Character: The Happy Prince (young man)

Oscar Wilde lived in England in the late 1800s and was a major playwright and novelist who influenced the writers of the time significantly. His work is still popular on the page and on the stage. Among his writings are a delightful collection of fairy tales. This selection comes from a story of a beautiful inspirational statue of a young prince in the square of a large city. All who pass the statue remark about how happy the young Prince looks and how envious they are of his contentment. A frisky swallow flies into the city, looking for his friends and discovers that they flew south six weeks earlier. The swallow is sad because of a failed love for the beautiful bird Reed. All alone, the swallow sleeps at the feet of the Happy Prince statue. When he feels drops of water hit his wings, he suspects rain. However, when he looks up, he sees that the statue, now very much alive, is crying.

In this speech, the Happy Prince tells the swallow why he cries.

"I am the Happy Prince."

["Why are you weeping then?" asked the Swallow, "You have quite drenched me."]

"When I was alive and had a human heart," [answered the statue,] "I did not know what tears were, for I lived in the Palace of Sans-Souci, where sorrow is not allowed to enter. In the daytime I played with my companions in the garden, and in the evening I led the dance in the Great Hall. Round the garden ran a very lofty wall, but I never cared to ask what lay beyond it, everything about me was so beautiful. My courtiers called me the Happy Prince, and happy indeed I was, if pleasure be happiness. So I lived, and so I died. And now that I am dead they have set me up here so high that I can see all the ugliness and the misery of my city, and though my heart is made of lead yet I cannot choose but weep."

["What! is he not solid gold?" said the Swallow to himself. He was too polite to make any personal remarks out loud.]

"Far away," [continued the statue in a low musical voice,] "far away in a little street there is a poor house. One of the windows is open, and through it I can see a woman seated at a table. Her face is thin and worn, and she has coarse, red hands, all pricked by the needle, for she is a seamstress. She is embroidering passion-flowers on a satin gown for the loveliest of the Queen's maids-of-honour to wear at the next Court-ball. In a bed in the corner of the room her little boy is lying ill. He has a fever, and is asking for oranges. His mother has nothing to give him but river water, so he is crying. Swallow, Swallow, little Swallow, will you not bring her the ruby out of my sword-hilt? My feet are fastened to this pedestal and I cannot move."

THE HAPPY TIME
by Samuel Taylor
Based on the Stories by Robert Fontaine

The Character: Bibi (12)

This play revolves around an exuberant French family, the Bonnards, living in Ottawa, Canada. Bibi Bonnard is on the verge of becoming a man, and everyone in the household, including his father, a good natured musician; Uncle Desmond, a fun-loving traveling salesman; Uncle Louis, who enjoys his wine, and Grandpère, who believes love allows one to live forever. Maman, Bibi's mother, attempts to keep these colorful characters in line with her calming manner but often fails. She is afraid that her men's behavior may not always be a good influence on Bibi, and when an unfortunate incident occurs at school, her fears appear real. Fortunately, the men rally behind Bibi and help him learn the value of truth.

In the speech excerpted below, Bibi tells what has happened to him at school when he was unfairly accused of drawing an inappropriate picture of a teacher.

BIBI: I will not go back to school! I will never go back to school! […] I didn't do it! It's not fair! […] Why do I have to tell lies to escape a beating? Why will no one believe the truth? […] I did not do it! […] In school, one finds a drawing in pencil, a dirty picture. A teacher finds it. They come to me. […] It is from *La Vie Parisienne,* which I have taken to school […] and trade it to a boy for baseball pictures. This is all I know. The next period, in English class, the teacher finds a drawing on the floor. It is on composition paper. It is copied in pencil from *La Vie Parisienne.* It is a picture of a girl standing like so. *(He illustrates with the traditional pose, feet apart, hands on hips, head back, laughing.)* […] But in this picture, on the head, instead of the face of the girl in the magazine, there is drawn the face of Miss Short, the geometry teacher. […] But also, with pencil, the rest of the clothes have been removed and many things have been added. […] I am taken to the principal's office. […] It is nobody's fault. Only Sally

O'Hare's. […] It is she who tells the teacher that I have brought the magazine to school. And then, in the principal's office, they ask her if I drew the picture and she says yes, I drew it. It is a lie! I did not draw it! […] Since yesterday, when she did not stay to eat…she kicks me, she trips me, she spills ink on my books. […] Why does she do this? […] *(He pulls down his stocking to show his shin.)* Look – black and blue! […] When I say it is true that I bring the magazine to school, but it is not true I draw the picture, the principal just laughs. He looks at me, and says he has heard about me and my family. […] He says he has heard that I have an uncle who drinks all his life and another uncle who chases after all the women and that my father is a crazy musician, so no wonder I am like I am and draw dirty pictures. […] The principal, Mr. Frye, says that I must come to him every day, and every day he will beat me until I tell the truth. But I have told the truth…! *(And again he is in tears.)* Grandpère says it is better to tell a lie, and escape the beating; that I should say I drew the picture, but [I think it is better to tell the truth!]

HEY LITTLE WALTER
by Carla Debbie Alleyne

The Character: Albert (12-14)

Carla Debbie Alleyne was sixteen when she wrote this one-act play and submitted it to the Foundation of the Dramatists Guild's annual Young Playwrights Festival. The play was one of six selected for production at the Playwrights Horizons in 1989. Set in a ghetto, the story revolves around little Walter, who, like so many other young boys in similar circumstances, seems to have no other hope of bettering his life except through selling drugs. Hope is found in the inspiration of Walter's sister, Latoya, who paints a picture at school of her dream – a family that is safe and together.

In the speech below, Walter's little brother, Albert, stands up for himself while pretending to shoot hoops.

ALBERT: S'up, Boys? Here I am, ready to play. *(Pause.)* What you laughing at? Yo, man, gimme time. Mama's gonna hook me up with some fly sneakers soon. *(Pause.)* Yo, what? Look, K mart happens to be a very popular store. Dag, man, why you always trying to diss? Now, if I told everybody your mom is on welfare, you'd get mad, right? Oh, so now you want to challenge me? You know I can dunk better than you. Aight, aight, I'll go first. *(Dribbles.)* Magic, watch out! *(Heads for Walter's hoop and trips.)* Damn these sneakers. *(Looks up.)* Yo, why yawl laughing? Stop laughing at me. You just wait and see. *(Runs off.)* Just wait and see.
(The music grows louder, blackout.)

THE LITTLE PRINCE
by Antoine de Saint Exupéry

The Characters: Little Prince (young boy)

An adult man, flying over the Sahara Desert, develops engine trouble
and is stranded. He tries desperately to fix his airplane. Soon, he
discovers a Little Prince from another planet, a planet not bigger than a
house. The Little Prince introduces himself and explains that he's
attempting to search the universe to discover the true meaning of life.

In the first speech, the Little Prince explains that he is both
perplexed and bewildered about how some facts of nature seem
unreasonable. He offers the pilot this argument for not trusting
appearances.

"I know a planet where there is a certain red-faced gentleman. He
has never smelled a flower. He has never looked at a star. He has never
loved anyone. He has never done anything in his life but add up
figures. And all day he says over and over, just like you: 'I am busy
with matters of consequence!' And that makes him swell up with
pride. But he is not a man – he is a mushroom!"

["A what?"

"A mushroom!"

The little prince was now white with rage.]

"The flowers have been growing thorns for millions of years. For
millions of years the sheep have been eating them just the same. And is
it not a matter of consequence to try to understand why the flowers go
to so much trouble to grow thorns which are never of any use to them?
Is the warfare between the sheep and the flowers not important? Is this
not of more consequence than a fat, red-faced gentleman's sums? And
if I know – I, myself – one flower which is unique in the world, which
grows nowhere but on my planet, but which one little sheep can
destroy in a single bite some morning, without even noticing what he is
doing – Oh! You think that is not important!"

[His face turned from white to red as he continued:]

"If someone loves a flower, of which just one single blossom grows
in all the millions and millions of stars, it is enough to make him happy
just to look at the stars. He can say to himself: 'Somewhere, my flower

is there...' But if the sheep eats the flower, in one moment all his stars will be darkened...And you think that is not important!"

In this second speech, the little Prince tells the pilot about a special flower that at first fascinated him and caused him to love it deeply, then it seemed to become selfish and demanding.

"I ought not to have listened to her," [he confided to me one day.] "I never ought to listen to the flowers. One should simply look at them and breathe their fragrance. Mine perfumed all my planet. But I did not know how to take pleasure in all her grace. This tale of claws, which disturbed me so much, should only have filled my heart with tenderness and pity."

[And he continued his confidences:]

"The fact is that I did not know how to understand anything! I ought to have judged by deeds and not by words. She cast her fragrance and her radiance over me. I ought never to have run away from her...I ought to have guessed all the affection that lay behind her poor little stratagems. Flowers are so inconsistent! But I was too young to know how to love her..."

The Character: The Fox

Along the way in his Earthly journey, the Little Prince meets a wise fox who helps him understand how special his flower was and who shares a secret about life.

"Nothing is perfect.

"My life is very monotonous. I hunt chickens; men hunt me. All the chickens are just alike, and all the men are just alike. And, in consequence, I am a little bored. But if you tame me, it will be as if the sun came to shine on my life. I shall know the sound of a step that will be different from all the others. Other steps send me hurrying back underneath the ground. Yours will call me, like music, out of my burrow. And then look: you see the grain-fields down yonder? I do not eat bread. Wheat is of no use to me. The wheat fields have nothing to say to me. And that is sad. But you have hair that is the color of gold. Think how wonderful that will be when you have tamed me! The grain, which is also golden, will bring me back the thought of you. And I shall love to listen to the wind in the wheat...

"Please – tame me!"

In this last speech, having arrived at the meaning of life, the Little Prince shares his feelings with the pilot.

"All men have the stars, but they are not the same things for different people. For some, who are travelers, the stars are guides. For others they are no more than little lights in the sky. For others, who are scholars, they are problems. For my businessman they were wealth. But all these stars are silent. You – you alone – will have the stars as no one else has them –"

["What are you trying to say?"]

"In one of the stars I shall be living. In one of them I shall be laughing. And so it will be as if all the stars were laughing, when you look at the sky at night...You – only you – will have stars that can laugh!

"And when your sorrow is comforted (time soothes all sorrows), you will be content that you have known me. You will always be my friend. You will want to laugh with me. And you will sometimes open your window, so, for that pleasure...And your friends will be properly astonished to see you laughing as you look up at the sky! Then you will say to them, 'Yes, the stars always make me laugh!' And they will think you are crazy. It will be a very shabby trick that I shall have played on you...

"It will be as if, in place of the stars, I had given you a great number of little bells that knew how to laugh..."

A LETTER FROM MOZART
Wolfgang Amadeus Mozart

Wolfgang Mozart (13)

The brilliant eighteenth-century composer Wolfgang Amadeus Mozart touched and fascinated the world with his wonderful music. He was also a great letter writer, beginning to write at an early age. As he traveled Europe, he sent home letters to his sister and mother (his father often accompanied him.) His letters offer us insights into his feelings and thoughts about the world and his experiences as a musician and composer. Here, he writes to his mother and sister from Bologna.

TO HIS MOTHER AND SISTER
Bologna, 21 August 1770

I too am still alive and, what is more, as merry as can be. I had a great desire today to ride on a donkey, for it is the custom in Italy, and so I thought that I too should try it. We have the honour to go about with a certain Dominican, who is regarded as a holy man. For my part I do not believe it, for at breakfast he often takes a cup of chocolate and immediately afterwards a good glass of strong Spanish wine; and I myself have had the honour of lunching with this saint who at table drank a whole decanter and finished up with a full glass of strong wine, two large slices of melon, some peaches, pears, five cups of coffee, a whole plate of cloves, and two full saucers of milk and lemon. He may, of course, be following some sort of diet, but I do not think so, for it would be too much; moreover he takes several little snacks during the afternoon. *Addio.* Farewell. Kiss Mamma's hands for me. My greetings to all who know me.

THIS BOY'S LIFE
by Tobias Wolff

The Character: Toby (10-11)

The author, now older, recalls a period in his life (1955) when he and his mother, divorced from the father, set out from Florida to Utah on their own. The book is filled with stories of the young Toby's fascinating, often touching, experiences in life and the close bond that develops between he and his mother. Disconnected as his life may be, troubled later by a harsh stepfather, Toby is restless as he adjusts to new situations and experiences. We see a young boy who is capable of both kindness and mischievousness.

In the first speech, Toby recalls a variation on archery practice that included some exciting risks.

I belonged to the Archery Club. Girls were free to join but none did. On rainy days we practiced in the church basement, on clear days outside. Sister James watched us when she could; at other times we were supervised by an older nun who was nearsighted and tried to control us by saying, "Boys, boys..."

The people next door kept cats. The cats were used to having the run of the churchyard and it took them a while to understand that they were no longer predators but prey – big calicoes and marmalades sitting in the sunshine, tails curled prettily around themselves, cocking their heads from side to side as our arrows zipped past. We never hit any of them, but we came close. Finally the cats caught on and quit the field. When this happened we began hunting each other.

Pretending to look for overshot arrows, we would drift beyond the targets to a stand of trees where the old nun couldn't see us. There the game began. At first the idea was to creep around and let fly in such a way that your arrow thunked into the tree nearest your quarry. For a time we were content to count this a hit. But the rule proved too confining for some, and then the rest of us had no choice but to throw it over too, as friends of mine would later throw over the rules governing fights with water balloons, rocks and BB guns.

The game got interesting. All of us had close calls, close calls that were recounted until they became legend. The Time Donny Got Hit in the Wallet. The Time Patrick Had His Shoe Shot Off. A few of the boys came to their senses and dropped out but the rest of us carried on. We did so in a resolutely innocent way, never admitting to ourselves what the real object was: that is, to bring somebody down. Among the trees I achieved absolute vacancy of mind. I had no thought of being hurt or of hurting anyone else, not even as I notched my arrow and pulled it back, intent on some movement in the shadows ahead. I was doing just that one afternoon, drawing my bow, ready to fire as soon as my target showed himself again, when I heard a rustling behind me. I spun around.

Sister James had been about to say something. Her mouth was open. She looked at the arrow I was aiming at her, then looked at me. In her presence my thoughtlessness forsook me. I knew exactly what I had been doing. We stood like that for a time. Finally I pointed the arrow at the ground. I unnotched it and started to make some excuse, but she closed her eyes at the sound of my voice and waved her hands as if to shoo away gnats. "Practice is over," she said. Then she turned and left me there.

In this second speech, Toby tells of a youthful success with two of his friends. Together they succeed in getting away with breaking windows and causing much trouble.

On Halloween, Taylor and Silver and I broke out some windows in the school cafeteria. The next day two policemen came to school and several boys with bad reputations were called out of class to talk to them. Nobody thought of us, not even of Taylor, who had a recorded history of window breaking. The reason nobody thought of us was that at school, in the presence of really tough kids who got into fights and talked back to teachers, we were colorless and mild.

At the end of the day the principal came on the public address system and announced that the guilty parties had been identified. Before taking action, however, he wanted to give these individuals a chance to come forward on their own. A voluntary confession now would work greatly in their favor later on. Taylor and Silver and I avoided looking at each other. We knew it was a bluff, because we'd been in the same classroom all day long. Otherwise, the trick would have worked. We didn't trust each other, and any suspicion that one of us was weakening would have created a stampede of betrayal.

We got away with it. A week later we came back after a movie to break some more windows, then chickened out when a car turned into the parking lot and sat there with its engine running for a few minutes before driving away.

Instead of making us more careful, the interest of the police in what we'd done elated us. We became self-important, cocksure, insane in our arrogance. We broke windows. We broke streetlights. We opened the doors of cars parked on hills and released the emergency brakes so they smashed into the cars below. We set bags of shit on fire and left them on doorsteps, but people didn't stamp them out as they were supposed to do; instead they waited with weary expressions as the bags burned, now and then looking up to scan the shadows from which they felt us watching them.

We did these things in darkness and in the light of day, moving always to the sound of breaking glass and yowling cats and grinding metal.

YOU'RE A GOOD MAN, CHARLIE BROWN

From the play script of a musical entertainment based on the comic strip, Peanuts *by Charles M. Schultz*
Music, lyrics, and adaptation by Clark Gesner

Character: Charlie Brown (boy)

Charles M. Schultz created a lovable set of characters that entertained the world in newspapers for years and year. Clark Gesner's truthful musical adaptation brought the characters to life on the stage and appealed to young and old alike. There is an ageless quality to these children (and one imaginative and frisky dog named Snoopy). The struggles of one Charlie Brown to be recognized in this life, the complications of friendships and relationships, the search for happiness and personal integrity, infuse this story. These are struggles that apply to people of all ages. Here, Mr. Schultz (with the help of Mr. Gesner) has given us all a genuine opportunity to laugh, and feel, and to maybe learn something. In this first speech, Charlie Brown, alone on the playground, sits with his sack lunch.

CHARLIE BROWN: I think lunchtime is about the worst time of the day for me. Always having to sit here alone. Of course, sometimes mornings aren't so pleasant, either-waking up and wondering if anyone would really miss me if I never got out of bed. Then there's the night, too-lying there and thinking about all the stupid things I've done during the day. And all those hours in between-when I do all those stupid things. Well, lunchtime is among the worst times of the day for me.

Well, I guess I'd better see what I've got. (*He opens the bag, unwraps a sandwich, and looks inside*) Peanut butter. (*He bites and chews*) Some psychiatrists say that people who eat peanut butter sandwiches are lonely. I guess they're right. And if you're really lonely, the peanut butter sticks to the roof of your mouth. (*He munches quietly, idly fingering the bench*) Boy, the PTA sure did a good job of painting these benches. (*He looks off to one side*) There's that cute little redhead girl eating her lunch over there. I wonder what she'd do if I went over and asked her if I could sit and have lunch with her. She'd probably laugh right in my face. It's hard on a face when it gets laughed in. There's an empty place next to her on the bench. There's no reason why I couldn't just go over and sit there. I could do that right now. All I have to do is stand up. (*He stands*) I'm standing up. (*He sits*) I'm sitting down. I'm a coward. I'm so much of a coward she wouldn't even think of looking at me. She hardly ever *does* look at me. In fact, I can't remember her ever looking at me. Why shouldn't she look at me? Is there a reason in the world why she shouldn't look at me? Is she so great and am I so small that she couldn't spare one little moment just to... (*He freezes*) She's looking at me. (*In terror he looks one way, then another*) She's *looking* at me. (*His head looks all around, frantically trying to find something else to notice. His teeth clench. Tension builds. Then, with one motion, he pops the paper bag over his head.*) Lunchtime is among the worst times of the day for me. If that little redheaded girl is looking at me with this stupid bag on my head she must think I'm the biggest fool alive. But if she isn't looking at me, then maybe I could take it off quickly and she'd never notice it. On the other hand, I can't tell if she's looking until I take it off. Then again, if I *never* take it off, I'll never have to know if she was looking or not. On the other hand, it's very hard to breathe in here. (*There is a moment of tense silence. Then his hand rises slowly, jerks the bag from his head and folds it quickly as he glances furtively in the direction of the little girl. He smiles*) She's not looking at me. (*He looks concerned*) I wonder why she never looks at me. (*The school bell jangles once again*) Oh well, another lunch hour over with. Only two thousand, eight hundred and sixty-three to go.

In this second speech, Charlie Brown tells of his newfound hope and "...confidence in the basic goodness of my fellow man."

CHARLIE BROWN: You know, I don't know if you'll understand this or not, but sometimes, even when I'm feeling very low, I'll see some little thing that will somehow renew my faith. Just something like that leaf, for instance-clinging to this tree in spite of wind and storm. You know, that makes me think that courage and tenacity are about the greatest values that a man can have.

Suddenly my old confidence is back and I know things aren't half as bad as I make them out to be. Suddenly I know that with the strength of his convictions a man can move mountains, and I can proceed with full confidence in the basic goodness of my fellow man. I know that now. I know it.

(*With unfamiliar strength in his step, Charlie Brown turns and makes his way off-stage, a glimmer of new hope in his eyes.*)

Character: Schroeder (boy)

Schroeder's constant shadow is the bold and brassy Lucy. Although she adores Schroeder and his brilliant piano playing, he doesn't respond. Here, Schroeder takes a moment to be extremely truthful with Lucy.

SCHROEDER: I'm sorry to have to say it right to your face, Lucy, but it's true. You're a very crabby person. I know your crabbiness has probably become so natural to you now that you're not even aware when you're being crabby, but it's true just the same. You're a very crabby person and you're crabby to just about everyone you meet. (*Lucy remains silent-just barely*) Now I hope you don't mind my saying this, Lucy, and I hope you'll take it in the spirit that it's meant. I think we should all be open to any opportunity to learn more about ourselves. I think Socrates was very right when he said that one of the first rules for anyone in life is "Know thyself." (*Lucy has begun whistling quietly to herself*) Well, I guess I've said about enough. I hope I haven't offended you or anything. (*He makes an awkward exit*)